A Mantis Carol

A MANTIS CAROL

LAURENS VAN DER POST

*'And always mantis would have a dream,'
they told me in the desert. 'And the dream
would show him what to do.'*

ISLAND PRESS

Washington, D.C. • Covelo, California

ISLAND PRESS is a trademark of The Center for Resource Economics.

Island Press edition published by arrangement with William Morrow and Company, Inc.

Library of Congress Cataloging-in-Publication Data

Van der Post, Laurens.
  A mantis carol.

  1. Taaibosch, Hans. 2. Bushmen. I. Title.
DT764.B8T258 973'.04'961 (B) 75-38552
ISBN 0-933280-21-1

Printed on recycled, acid-free paper

Manufactured in the United States of America

Published in Great Britain in 1975 by The Hogarth Press Ltd.
Published in the United States in 1976 by William Morrow
        and Company, Inc.
Island Press edition: fifth printing December 1994.

To the memory of Martha Jaeger
as well as MAT who was in prison with me
and left it for such a walk-about, spirit
unembittered, and heart intact.

CONTENTS

PREAMBLE

Preamble

THIS is a true story which may well appear stranger than fiction, since the truth unhappily, from the point of view of those who try to serve it, is always more than literal or statistical fact. Indeed, the writer who would warm such cold, literal and statistical clay with life finds himself inevitably involved in some sort of alchemical approach to his subject, since life and the living of it for all our knowing, is still as great a mystery at its end as it was in its beginning. As fast as our knowledge expands to the rim of the unknown, the mystery at heart forms another horizon compelling the known to keep to the same respectful distance again.

None of this atmosphere of mystery which may preside over this story, therefore, is any of my intention or invention, but something imposed on me by the nature of the living pattern with which this story is concerned, and the task of making it live for others as it lived for me. Though I have tried to tell it with due respect for its literal and statistical fact, an air of the mysterious must remain because of the inevitable limitation of words in expressing the inexpressible. Awareness and articulation, despite the logic of positivism and the philosophy of semantics, are not synonymous. Each one of us is aware of far more than he can ever express. We all know more than we allow ourselves to know because of a cer-

11

tain cowardice in face of the inexpressible, and fear of accepting its effect on us as guide to the nature of its reality. Yet those who can persuade themselves to be guided thus in their pursuit of the totality of truth find themselves rewarded not so much by a surrender of any significant part of the essential mystery, as by its transformation into something accessible as living wonder.

None the less, whether mystery or wonder, this element present in the events recorded here is so strong that it is necessary to stress that the people concerned in the telling are not imaginary but real. I have even used their own names whenever possible, and suppressed and changed them only when I have not known them or thought I might give embarrassment.

Above all, Hans Taaibosch is the name under which the principal character came into the story. To my everlasting regret, I could not discover the name I suspect he must have had originally. Yet I underline the fact that I used the one name by which he was known in the slight hope that somewhere, someone may possibly remember how he came to get it and, even if incapable of telling us more than that about him, may be grateful for this opportunity to give him the salute he merits as he is dismissed for the last time from his own ground of parade as a private soldier of life who served it, I believe, far above and beyond the call of duty.

THE COMING OF MANTIS

The Coming of Mantis

ALTHOUGH this story is as complete as anything can ever be in an human awareness bound to its miniscule ration of life in the here and now, I still have only to think of it to find it as mysterious as some midnight visitation. Yet none of this was apparent to me for a long time. The beginning in itself appeared a trivial part of the routine traffic of my working life and I did not imagine at the time that it could possibly possess any extraterritorial connections for me. Insignificant as it was, so without obvious substance of any special import that it corresponded almost to the Euclidian definition of a point as that which has no size or magnitude but only position, I did not realize then as I do now, that position in mind and spirit as well as within the unfolding process of our expanding universe, is more important than size or I might have taken greater notice of the event. I might have realized that even on such an intangible scale something extra-ordinary was moving into position in my life, had I taken heed of some of the coincidences which followed the positioning and accompanied its evolution.

This was perhaps the most reprehensible lapse of all, for some instinct has prevented me from ever finding coincidences accidental. I had come gradually to think of them as manifestations of some cosmic law of which we are inadequately aware, confirming among many other

15

things, the extent to which one's own life was obedient to an overwhelming universal pattern. I had even reached at that precise moment the place in the book I was writing where I was trying to suggest that this great veiled law with its special messengers of strange, often absurd parallels disturbing our highly organized allegiance to a rational and causal progression of things, could be the law governing the growth of meaning in our lives, the kind of meaning which the Chinese centuries before Christ defined as that which has always existed through itself. I can only excuse the lapse by the fact that I was working hard on the successor to my book *The Lost World of the Kalahari*, which meant even more to me and which was growing too slowly for my liking from the seed of its title, *The Heart of the Hunter*.

My apprenticeship to the cause of the theme of these two books had been long and hard. I had just behind me, for instance, nearly five years of exploration of the great known, unknown of the Kalahari desert of southern Africa, including a long expedition into the heart of that great wasteland to find some remnants of the vanished first people of my native country, the Bushmen of southern Africa, in order not only to live with them but also to learn from them. As a result my life and mind were so conditioned as to have room for little else, when as I now see it, the story began to probe so unobtrusively for its own position in my life.

When the letter which started it all arrived from America, I put it on one side for ten days before opening it, so incapable did I feel of finding a place in my mind for its contents. In case this sounds exaggerated, I may add that a few letters a day from friends and people one loves may be a joy but at such a moment, the twenty to thirty envelopes that came through my door each morning were a form of torture. When I came at last reluctantly to open this particular letter it was not without feelings of guilt which made me overlook the fact that its contents also coincided with what I was doing.

The letter was from an unknown woman in New York. She asked if I could help her to understand an image which had recurred in her dreams over many years. In the last five years it had recurred with increasing frequency and indeed, at the time of writing her letter, was happening almost nightly. She said that she was an analytical psychologist and had learned from her vocation that human beings neglected their dreams, particularly recurring dreams, at their peril. Accordingly she had given all the understanding of which she was capable to determine the purpose of this recurrent image. This image was always that of a praying mantis. She had, she declared, never seen a praying mantis, but when the dream came to her she had read all she could about them and looked up illustrations in libraries and allusions to them in literature, but could discover nothing whatsoever to account for the appearance in her dreaming mind of an insect she had never encountered or given any conscious thought to.

She had consulted eminent colleagues in the United States, London and Zürich and even a great Zen Buddhist scholar in Japan whom, although I did not know it then, I was to meet with her in the course of the progression of this story.

Her failure to arrive at some understanding of the phenomenon, despite the efforts of all these years, implied that it must be a totally haphazard, random and meaningless intrusion in the imagery of her spirit. This was the truly agonizing aspect of it all which haunted her more and more, because it challenged a basic axiom of

17

her faith and made a nonsense of her considerable experience of human psychology. Nothing, however trivial or absurd its appearance, she believed, could possibly come up unbidden out of the darkness of the human mind, as this praying mantis had done, without carrying a charge of as yet unrecognized meaning peculiarly its own, seeking flesh and blood, brave and caring enough to live it.

She was in despair until two months before writing, when someone from Japan sent her a book of mine on Africa. She read it with a strange absurd feeling of having been there already, and noted with a sudden inrush of hope all that I had written about the praying mantis, and how it had once been called 'the god of the Hottentots of Africa' but in reality had been, and still was, the god of the Bushmen of southern Africa. Could I perhaps help her to find some understanding of this dream theme conducted in her sleeping self by a praying mantis that refused to go away? She signed herself Martha Jaeger.

Since this is not fiction but a true story I give her real name. She is not only dead and cannot be embarrassed by any personal references, but also I am certain, having come to know her well, that she would not have resented mention of her name since it was significant within itself and constituted another of those coincidences which I ignored at the time.

I take her surname first because it is the name she was born to and it represents as nearly as a single word can all the life immemorial that had gone into the making of her as the woman she was. Jaeger is the German for hunter. No name could ever have suited her nature better. The hunter in human imagination everywhere serves as a plenipotentiary of that part of the human personality which is always, whether we know it or not, in search of new and greater meaning. That is why I believe, for instance, we are so moved when Baudelaire, in what is perhaps the finest of his poems, speaks of art as a call on the horn of hunters lost in the great woods.

Martha Jaeger was a born and, to the end of her life, a dedicated hunter in this sense, not of big game but of great meaning. Moreover, the Bushman for whom the mantis of which she was constantly dreaming was god, was and is, in the purest and most exclusive use of the term, a hunter. And yet there I was staring at the name of Jaeger on my desk in the process of writing a book called *The Heart of the Hunter*, thinking only with a sigh of regret that I would have to make time now to answer yet another letter.

Then there was her own private and personal name, Martha. The first Martha, as Kipling in a poem devoted to her implies so poignantly even if not without characteristic extravagance, was the mother of sons condemned to work in darkness, unlike the sons of Mary who were children of the light. The Bushmen metaphorically were sons of Martha, destined to live in the darkness of a dark continent despite the bright light of its day, long before even the first Martha was born. A woman who was after a fashion to mother this story, therefore, could hardly have been more appropriately named.

At that moment of intense preoccupation, however, none of this had the clear outline for me that it so obviously possessed all along as I realize now, seeing it in the focus of a backward glance invested with the power of magnification given to a sense of final valediction, and the clarity of the autumnal nostalgia of an African self-exiled in Europe, as acute as any physical pain. But something of the potential significance of it all must have found a chink in my preoccupation because I wrote to her at length in the end and invited more by asking her for detailed examples of the dreams over which mantis presided.

Accordingly, despite myself, I got involved in a correspondence with this Martha Jaeger which became more and more animated as I began to gather, from her responses, how what I was telling her of the praying mantis and its role in the imagination and life of the Bushman was producing an objective confirmation of what I already suspected; this particular pattern of the imagination of the despised, most cruelly persecuted and almost exterminated Bushman of southern Africa, was not only of subjective importance to him and me but also mattered to an understanding of the nature of human imagination everywhere. His conscious mind corresponded in some sort to our dreaming selves and accordingly was one of the clearest mirrors accessible to us today for reflecting imponderables of meaning, that surfaced unbidden in unfamiliar images, as Martha Jaeger's mantis had done, from the unconscious of the most sophisticated mind of the desperate world of today, seeking apparently to inform it of an unknown and profoundly rejected self. Could it not be that by rendering it in a contemporary idiom, what was first and last in life which have become so brutally separated and pitted against each other in our spirit today, could be reconciled and joined again to give us back our feeling of continuity, the loss of which seemed to me the main cause of the profound sense of isolation and lack of purpose making a fragment of our own little day? Could it not perhaps also serve to mend and make whole the fracture of the spirit of our time, as it appeared to be doing so impressively for Martha Jaeger and all the people who came to her for help?

I am compelled to leave it at that, in the form of a

The Coming of Mantis

question, because I had no answers to match it then, and both question and general observation in the consequences of my correspondence with Martha Jaeger which prompted it, are illustration enough of how significant a direction it took despite myself. As for the details of her recurrent dream, although she is dead, I do not feel, with one exception, that I have a right to speak of them, nor do I believe that, significant as they are in themselves, they are relevant to the story.

What does matter is that she came from America specially to a symposium in which I was taking part at the annual Eranos gathering in the Casa Gabriella on Lake Maggiore in the late summer of a fateful year. We were able to talk there in a way for which no letters, however articulate, can ever be an adequate substitute. As a result I, who am not a psychologist and who had no personal experience of psychological analysis, was able to pass on to her, purely from what I had experienced of the role of the praying mantis in a living society, something that transformed into a source of revelation a dream pattern which had seemed so meaningless as to pose a grave threat to her faith in her vocation. It changed, she said, the whole course of her being.

The change was confirmed on her return home by another mantis dream; the exception to the rule of silence in this regard which I mentioned. She dreamt that she was walking barefoot through the green-gold grass of the evening of the last day of a great summer. She looked down in the yellow light of a setting sun and there was mantis, sitting firmly and happily in position in the middle of her right foot where her toes joined it.

The dream was as short as this but extraordinarily vivid and broke into her sleep with such force that she woke up. Instead of feelings of confusion and at times alarm

21

produced in her by mantis's previous dream appearance, she was filled on this occasion with an indescribable sense of well-being and a re-belonging to life, happier than she had ever felt before. And immediately, lying there alone in the dark in her room, overlooking the great Hudson River so full of stars trembling on the brink of the fall of the year, that it flowed like another Milky Way in its own canyon of the night, between the skyscraper cliffs of New York, she felt as if she were with me by some camp-fire at night in the Kalahari Desert, listening again to a Bush-man story I had once told her of how mantis loved to sit between the toes of the black, patent-leather foot of the eland, which is the biggest, most powerful and yet also the gentlest and most civilized of antelopes in Africa.

She remembered how I described the eland foot to her, how it was made to expand and the toes to part as it came down on the red desert sand, preventing it from sinking in too deep for the comfort of the eland's going, and how as the majestic antelope lifted its foot, the toes would snap together with a sharp, electric click. Often, lying in the shade of some black storm tree or green camel thorn in the desert, I had listened to the sounds of a herd of eland grazing around me, the delicate and precise mag-netic click making music of magic for me, until I was able to understand not rationally but emotionally why the image of a god, even one presented as a mere insect, would have to take its position by some quirk of being as the one from which this kind of electricity issued, in order to direct a particular morsel of mortal flesh and blood in the way it wished to go.

She remembered how the eland was the favourite food not only for the body but also for the imagination of the hunters of the desert. I had told her how one had only to look at the portraits of the eland they painted and which

22

The Coming of Mantis

still glow in the purple shadows of some hidden canvas of rock or smooth overhang of cliff in southern Africa, to see that it was rendered with a care and a love given to no other animal, and raised to a stature that was almost mystical. One had just to hear them talking about the eland to notice that whenever his name came up their voices had what I described to her as a special eland note. The greatest and most evocative of all their songs was their eland song, full and overflowing with a nostalgia not for some particular plot of earth so much as for the source from where life itself had come. One of the greatest of all their dances, greater even than their fire dance, was the eland dance, and they would explain all this by saying that of all the animals in the world, that dearest to mantis's heart was the eland.

I had told her therefore that it would seem as if mantis had placed himself between the toes of the eland as a deliberate sign, almost a first commandment to the Bushman spirit, that they must follow all that the eland evoked in their minds and hearts in order to walk in the way of their god. Besides had I not also stressed how mantis himself was a great dreamer? Whenever in doubt or in trouble he would dream a dream and the dream would see him through, so much so that a Bushman hunter had told me one day, his dark antique eyes amber with inrush of light, 'You see, there is a dream dreaming us.'

Remembering all this and more, she wrote to me that she had no doubt that the appearance of mantis in such a position in her dream was a sign that she was restored to her natural self and after the summer of her life was bound again on her own lawful occasion in time. For what could be more natural — the interpretation implied in the question was hers and not mine — than to kick off one's shoes and walk barefoot again through perennial grass, with one's direction in the keeping of what she accepted now as one of the purest, natural images of the highest meaning men call God or, as I had once described mantis to her, the voice of the infinite in the small.

No doubt since mantis was as near to a first image of meaning as a modern mind could get, she had only just started out on a way that would be long. She had no idea where it would take her, but the joy of it was that an arrested part of herself was on its way again.

She never dreamt of mantis again, because we commented on the fact whenever we met. I was with her for nine consecutive days almost until the hour of her death some ten years later and mantis had not yet reappeared in any of her dreams although he had figured a great deal in her thinking. She had not dreamt of him again, she would say, totally unperturbed over this apparent desertion, because it was no longer necessary to dream of him.

But on this particular night of his last dream appearance, she had hardly come to the conclusion that followed on the parallel of the Bushman story of mantis sitting between the toes of the Kalahari eland, when she knew that she must write and ask me to come to America and talk more to her and her friends about all these Stone-Age manifestations that had made so great a difference to her spirit.

She got up early, so great was her feeling of urgency, and wrote and asked me to come. Outwardly, her request could not have come at a more awkward moment. I was progressing far too slowly for my liking with *The Heart of the Hunter*. She might have done with mantis and his friends, but I was having increasing difficulties with the lot of them. Just as she had been so certain, despite all appearances to the contrary, that nothing meaningless could issue spontaneously out of the dark in men, I was convinced that everything invested with a role however obscure or trivial in the myths, legends and stories of the Bushman likewise must have a specific meaning.

Mantis in particular could only have been chosen as the image of their greatest value because no other would have served as well. I had a feeling that all together these creations of Bushman imagination constituted an ancient, hieroglyphic code of great primary import and if only I could find the key to the cypher used in the encoding, I would uncover a most immediate message of vital significance. I believed that in order to do so I would have to discover, as it were, the human and contemporary psychological equivalents of the role this long and crowded procession of animals, birds, reptiles and insects played in Bushman imagination and society, before I would be able to crack the code, as to some extent we already appeared to have done with mantis in Martha Jaeger's dreams. But, even knowing these insects and animals almost personally, it was neither as easy nor as obvious as it might sound.

What, for instance, was one to make of a god who was an insect, yet married to a rock rabbit, as was mantis? What of their son who was neither animal, reptile nor insect, but something as intangible as a compound of elements of the rainbow which appeared divinely arched over the desert after one of its rare, miraculous storms of rain? What of the fact that this rainbow element was married and had as improbable a wife as a porcupine? On the face of it, all seemed the sheer nonsense my countrymen had judged it to be for centuries, and there were times when I doubted myself and wondered whether this strange dream material from an age of stone, however meaningful it had been in the beginning, might not now be incapable of total redemption into a contemporary idiom. I was afraid that if I took off even one day from my work I would lose heart as well as rhythm and that my only hope of success was to inch my way forward day by day without interruption as I had tried to do for so long already.

My inclination, therefore, was to say no at once, but I hesitated out of respect for Martha Jaeger and the meaning she had been able to extract from the appearance of the enigmatic mantis in her own imagination. So I waited and gave the matter a great deal of thought. It was as well that I did so, because from the moment I received her invitation my work refused to move on at all. I sat down at my writing table every morning as usual, hoping that I would be able to uncover the sentences necessary for pressing on again. Nothing at all came, for all my willing to the contrary. There seemed to be a complete block in my imagination, and, if that were so, experience suggested that I should stop forcing the pace and give my imagination the time necessary for some sort of resolution to grow out of it as it had never failed to do before. There appeared no reason therefore why I should not spend this period of waiting on a process that would become outside my control if I accepted the invitation, and on doing a number of things in the United States and Canada which I had promised all sorts of friends over the years I would do at the first moment an opportunity arose.

THE PLACE AND THE SEASON

The Place and the Season

I LEFT for America therefore as soon as possible by sea and was astonished and reassured to find that, somehow, mantis and his friends had set sail with me. The crossing of the stormy Western Ocean, far from setting us apart or merely holding us at the incomprehensible arm's length where I had left them when I ceased writing, seemed to draw us closer together. Many years later I was to meet someone who had travelled with me at the time and almost the first thing he asked me was whether I was still so preoccupied with all those strange birds, beasts, animals, insects and reptiles of Africa as I had been on that voyage. Apparently I had talked of little else to him. But perhaps even more reassuring was that the timing of my arrival in America seemed right and corresponded so closely to my own time within.

I arrived in New York in the early fall. The fall in America has always been something very special to me. It is one of the two natural phenomenon in the northern hemisphere that have always stirred me most. The other, of course, is the spring in England. Great as my love is for my own part of Africa and my tendency to set whatever it offers above all else in the world, I had long since to admit to myself that it is not equipped to rehearse the annual progression through time of all living, growing and even inanimate things as well as it is ordered in

A Mantis Carol

England and America. We have nothing that can measure up to the stature of an English spring, dressing up a naked world for the festival of summer. We have nothing so awesome as the fire of autumn sweeping through the great maple forests of America, stripping their leaves from them in tongues of flame until they stand naked and penitent before the reckoning we call winter. It is a moment always full of a profound and natural sanctity for me, when the earth round about me becomes like an antique temple wherein this conflagration, aflame and aflicker among the trees, accomplishes the final metamorphosis that fire did for the dead in those archaic places of the great forgotten mysteries, removing what was provisional, false and perishable from the spent life, so that only what was permanent, true and imperishable could accompany the spirit that once invested it on the journey to whatever lies beyond the here and the now.

It is almost as if in the fall everything around me there suddenly becomes allegorical and each tree represents some prodigal being, its inheritance spent in a summer of celebration, standing bankrupt before the great impartial necessities and recognizing for the first time that where it started from was the home to which it inevitably must return, and the bleak rounding journey about to begin without comfort, since any promise of reward of some unimagined increase in that inexhaustible place of origin comes to us all, always disguised as a fear of retribution.

I was not worried because such a view of my surroundings stood long condemned as the 'great pathetic fallacy'. The pathos and the error for me were in the reductive approach so deeply rooted in our slanted, one-sided age, that it is unaware of the profound interdependence of world without and world within and so fails to see how

30

life achieves brief, immortal moments only in the recognition of our role as the natural subjects of this great condominium. Whoever looked within his own troubled heart, stripped of preconception and prejudice, as those trees around me were being stripped of their leaves of flame, I believed, would find the frontiers between the two abolished and a gateway without gate giving on a world without end.

I felt I could say this with unusual certainty because the human spirit seemed to me whether we like it or not, to be within itself profoundly seasonal and that it would have been astonishing if in the annual progression of the seasons even the least imaginative of us did not recognize some sort of family connection with the immense wheeling round of birth, life, death and rebirth, to which not only our bodies but the pattern within that gives them their meaning are irrevocably bound. And since the deepest part of this pattern to me seemed one of prodigal departure and return, the earth of America, devout in the grip of one of the greatest falls I had ever seen, for me just then was parable earth.

I could not therefore have found the time less out of joint. I felt utterly synchronized to the season without and through this feeling of synchronicity, achieved a heightening of perception, enabling me to hope that my own imagination labouring on the almost incomprehensible trail of a mere insect travelling through ages of stone was being obedient to its own pattern of departure and return. Indeed this feeling of unexpected harmony between my own season and the fall of the year became a kind of fortress wherein the theme conducted by mantis was not only kept intact but was enabled to evolve despite the distractions of the long journey that followed, in a way and at a pace I believe now would not have been

31

possible if I had stayed at home. It was yet another demonstration of how a journey to new places in the physical
world can encourage a journey within to places where
the mind has not been before. The demonstration was
all the more striking because I could not even help the
theme along to the limited extent I would have done, had
I been able to go immediately to talk about it as I had
contracted to do with Martha Jaeger and her friends.

I had first to go north by rail to perform numbers of
other exacting and totally unrelated engagements. The
details of them are not important to the story except that
some serve as examples of how I was protected by this
natural correspondence between my own season and the
fall without. Although I was forced to give my mind to
things that could not have been more remote outwardly
from my deepest preoccupation, and there were weeks
wherein I seemed to have forgotten it utterly, the theme
itself never forgot me. Called or not called, mantis and
his friends were always there, travelling the improbable
miles with me.

And oh, what miles they were! I went from New
York to Montreal, Montreal to Kingston, and Kingston
to Toronto, giving lectures at universities and address-
ing meetings, although I have an intense dislike of speaking in public. From there I went out and on to
the great prairies and not only initiated a festival of arts
in Manitoba but talked and exposed myself for ten long
days to a process of question and answer from some of
the most enquiring young people in the world. From the
prairies I had to go on down south to San Francisco,
Berkeley, Los Angeles, San Diego and across the desert
to Texas and New Orleans, and then up to Washington.
Only then did I get to my main destination in New York.

So much travelling and so much else to do should have

obliterated all traces of the mantis trail in my imagination but last thing at night and first thing in the morning, in far too many ways to be recalled, it did not only remind me of itself but would suddenly present me with some slight new facet of comprehension of the incomprehensible. For instance, there was the night in my sleeper in Canada when I woke up and suddenly knew why a god-like mantis who brought fire to Stone-Age man had to have a son who was a compound of rainbow elements. Fire is our greatest image of consciousness on earth; the son mantis's future self, and the rainbow natural testimony of the striving of the human spirit to raise consciousness to a heavenly principle since as refraction of the white light of day into its constituent colours, it is a visualization of the discriminating, analytical element of the conscious spirit. That was its role in the Old Testament for Noah after the flood, the arc of man's first covenant with his highest meaning; it was so for Goethe and here it was so for Stone-Age man as well and the blessed, reassuring sense of continuity it brought to me that night was sweeter than sleep in that overland train speeding on towards the Rocky Mountains. In Winnipeg, shaving in the morning, I understood how such a son could only have been married to a porcupine, for the porcupine knew its way through the dark as no other wasteland animal did and had a nose for what was invisible and far away ahead that made it an appropriate image of the feminine intuitive element, the golden Ariadne thread of the human spirit which leads life through a maze of unawareness to an increase of consciousness.

Somewhere in New Mexico I understood why mantis had to love such a porcupine woman even more than his own rock rabbit wife because in such a role she was the image of his own inner objective self, his feminine soul in search of new and greater meaning. By the time I got to Texas my understanding appeared so widened that parallels between the myth of mantis, Greek mythology, our biblical story and the symbolism of our own time were lengthening and multiplying with a speed that was as startling as it was hair-raising.

But perhaps from the point of view of a world inclined to accept the evidence only of what is visible and physically demonstrable, the most striking vindication occurred when I arrived in Houston. I had never been to Houston. I had not met my hostess before although I had corresponded with her a great deal. She came to meet me at the railway station and drove me to her lovely home outside the city where it stood in ample wild grounds, a tall wood at the back, hung with lichen and soft with moss, as it declined towards a bayou of its own. As I helped her out of the car she took the key for the front door from her bag and turned towards it.

Instantly she drew back in alarm, gasping, 'What on earth is that sitting there?'

I looked. There, in an attitude of profound contemplation, as if waiting for a temple door to open, sat a large praying mantis. I told her what it was. Amazed, she said that although she and her husband had lived there for a great many years she had not seen a praying mantis there or anywhere else before. Even if I had any doubts left about the wisdom of undertaking the journey I think that this appearance of mantis in person on the scene might finally have removed them, so sure was I from then on that I was travelling as it were under his auspices.

Happily that was no longer necessary and the incident served only to accelerate the process of a resolution, and I eventually arrived in New York on 13th December,

The Place and the Season

which was my birthday, to begin my series of meetings with Martha Jaeger and her friends, with the code apparently broken and mantis's message come through to me with penetrating immediacy. I remember feeling in that regard too how singular and right the timing had continued to be. As I caught my first glimpse of the approaches to the great Hudson River again after all those weeks I noticed how the fall was accomplished, the fire drawn and the world white, silent and still before the coming of winter. I remembered the metaphor of my mind turning right over and thinking as I looked at the naked earth how like a great ship it was with sails tightly furled, hatches battened down, all that was loose and out of place firmly lashed to the decks or stowed away and all as ready as forethought and imagination could make it for the storms of wind and ice and snow about to be thrown against it. It was as if nature, aware that a great moment of truth was about to descend upon it, was exhorting all in its keeping by example to prepare likewise. In a way that now seems over egotistical I assumed that my role in this moment was confined to holding on to what was true in my own preoccupation, but I was about to learn that it possessed implications in a dimension I had not contemplated.

For six days then Martha Jaeger and her friends and I met at various places to talk about the Bushman, his nature and ways, his myths, legends and stories and above all the role of mantis in Stone-Age imagination. We started with a meeting in a large hall attended by a thousand or more people. We had smaller, more specialized meetings in her own apartment overlooking the Hudson River where one of those incredible suspension bridges at which America excels arches over the vast stretch of water as

35

easily as a pebble in flight. But the main and longest sessions were held at the Quaker training centre at Pendle Hill just outside Philadelphia.

Martha Jaeger at that time was Chairman of the Conference on Religion and Psychology of the Society of Friends and it seemed natural and right that most of our work should be done in this secluded and calm Quaker establishment in its beautiful and natural setting. Yet no matter where the meetings were held and who came to them, I was struck how without exception people who not only had never been to Africa but had never heard of the Bushman before, related to him instantly and followed this evolution of his imagination as if they themselves were utterly at home within it, all sitting like children in a Stone-Age nursery listening to their very first story told for the first time. At the end the nature of the theme and our joint effort at interpreting it, produced so great a sense of human totality and belonging also to life on the earth when it itself was young, that someone could only contain the emotion of the moment by reaching out at the truth in jest and declaring that we must be the first conference of Bushmen ever held in the United States of America.

Perhaps the most striking illustration of the union of diversity achieved came at one of the more intimate meetings at Martha Jaeger's apartment attended by Daisetzu Suzuki, the great Zen Buddhist teacher who was a friend of hers and to whom there has already been an oblique reference. There in the course of a discussion about many things he told me how he found mantis one of the most striking images he had ever encountered of one of the great Zen articles of faith; that of action through non-action and how he had already recommended this aspect of its meaning to Martha Jaeger. This of course too was more valuable confirmation that I was pursuing not merely an eccentric and purely subjective interest but one charged with objective meaning. And I would enlarge on it for its own sake were it not enough to illustrate how the impact of my unfamiliar theme on a new world, so remote from the Africa in which it had its source, could produce the consequences with which this story is concerned. That phase of the story, so long a mere potential, to use the unemotive language of physics, suddenly became kinetic on the last night at Pendle Hill.

ENVOY EXTRAORDINARY

Envoy Extraordinary

I HAD already noticed in the audience an attractive woman whom I took to be in her middle thirties. She was always dressed with more regard to the claims of fashion which the Society of Friends tended to disown. She had come to every meeting and always sat in the same chair in the third row from the front dressed with that gift so many American women possess of never appearing creased or crumpled, no matter how great the crush or long the journey. Also she was one of the few people who never asked any questions. She sat and listened intent, her wide eyes alert and a certain excess of stillness in her attitude, suggesting that she might be in the grip of a powerful and mounting excitement over a concern peculiarly her own.

Once or twice I thought she was about to stand up and ask a question but always, so it seemed to me, she was held back by an inhibition greater even than her impulse to speak. As a result I found myself observing her more and more closely until I accepted that what I was saying mattered more to her at that moment than to anybody else in the hall, even Martha Jaeger, and I was drawn to speak as it were through her, as a kind of amplifier for the rest of the hundreds who were there. I think an instinctive realization of this enabled her to overcome great and complex diffidences in what I was soon to

41

discover was an extremely sensitive, shy, fastidious and introverted nature.

At the end of our last meeting at Pendle Hill, instead of disappearing into the night as she had usually done, I found her waiting at the door to ask me in a low, tentative voice whether she could speak to me alone. I looked back at the now almost empty hall and thought of suggesting that we should find a chair there and talk together for a few minutes before I had to return to New York, but she knew instantly what was in my mind and exclaimed with some alarm, 'Oh not here, please! There are so many people coming in and out and I'm afraid it's rather a long story and will take a long time. You couldn't possibly let me drive you back to New York and we could talk as we went along. I know it's a lot to ask but I would be so grateful. It's so terribly important, not so much for me as for him.'

I had no idea who the 'him' could possibly be. She had come to all the meetings unattended. Yet there was something about the tone of her voice which, added to all that preceded the moment, convinced me that I couldn't possibly say no. I had already promised to drive back to New York with some friends. But so impressed was I by her own feeling of urgency that I instantly went to make my excuses to them and returned to go with her to her car.

It was late and we walked between the darkened buildings and past the great old barn, which had long since surpassed its original uses and now served as one of the favourite meeting places of the Society of Friends for the most devout of their purposes. It was strange how it loomed above us under the brilliant winter starlight like some granary of fate.

'You said it was important to you and to him. Is he joining us for the journey back?' I asked.

'Oh no,' she exclaimed, taken aback with reason as I was only to discover later. 'He's not. It's too late for that, but I wish he could have done so because I'm certain he would have given anything to meet you. He must have been so lonely although I only realize it now.'

She paused. I did not say anything because I felt that with so delicately balanced a personality one could not press or pry but had to wait for questions and answers to produce themselves of their own accord in their own good time. And indeed a process of question and answer did begin before long although still somewhat obscurely and certainly most obliquely.

'Does the name Hans Taaibosch convey anything to you?' she asked.

'If you mean in the sense that I have known anyone of that name it does not, but in other ways it has not meanings so much as a lot of associations for me,' I told her, somewhat startled to hear such a name in such a setting.

'Oh please tell me what they are!' She pressed instantly but there was no mistaking a mixture of disappointment and excitement in her voice; disappointment I imagined because I did not know anybody of that name and yet excitement also as it was not utterly meaningless to me as she had obviously, not without good reason, feared it could be.

We had just reached her car and I quickly opened the door for her. Since it was so cold I urged her, 'Won't you jump in and let me tell you what I can as we go along.'

I closed the door, walked round the back of the car and I remember that, as I did so, I looked up deep into the frosty night. I had never seen any sky anywhere in the northern hemisphere so packed with stars, and the stars themselves so large, clear and their light so precise and active. It was the nearest northern equivalent I had ever experienced to an African desert sky, and that perhaps was another reason why as I got into my seat I felt that I was only technically in America but quintessentially far away in the heart of some winter wasteland of the Kalahari. For all the miles in-between, my heart just then seemed bound not so much from the outskirts of one great American city to another but from one camp to another, where someone with that odd name of Taaibosch would not have been out of place. A certain awe derived from the incongruities of this and many other related subtleties of feeling silenced me. We drove for perhaps a mile or two until she had to remind me that I had not yet told her what the name Hans Taaibosch meant to me.

'Well as I have already explained,' I began, wondering if my words could go gently enough through an area that was obviously of such tender concern to her, 'I have never met anybody of that name and therefore could not have known your Hans Taaibosch. But what I can say without doubt is that a person with such a name could only have been a native of South Africa and a countryman of mine. Hans is as common a Christian name in South Africa as it is in Germany. But what is more unusual is the surname, Taaibosch. That is an Afrikaans name for one of the toughest plants in the country; a shrub which not only survives but remains green throughout the severest of the many severe droughts we get on an average every three years in South Africa.

'The term is in fact a compound of two words, *taai* which means tough in all the sense associated with the word in English except that it has a nuance of toughness to the point of indestructibility not found in the Anglo-Saxon equivalent. The other word, *bosch* is of course the

Afrikaans word for shrub or small bush in the South African-English sense of the word.'

'Oh, how good! I'm so glad. He couldn't possibly have been better named,' she interrupted with such obvious pleasure that it seemed cruel to add what I had to say.

'But I'm afraid that apt as this name appears to have been for your friend it probably was not his original name.' I went on with all the solicitude that I could manage. 'It sounds to me very like the kind of name my countrymen some generations ago bestowed on coloured people of the Cape whose surnames they either found too difficult to pronounce or did not think important enough to acknowledge. I'm afraid it is just one of those indications of our historical disregard for the identity and personal validity of the indigenous peoples of Africa. I'm glad to say it is changing today but there was a time not long ago when names of this kind were applied as a matter of arbitrary course to all Africans in European employ and even more commonly to Euro-Africans who had no tribal coherence or racial integrity to protect them. I would assume therefore that your Hans Taaibosch was some coloured person. No, not coloured in the American sense but in the special South African one which denotes someone of mixed indigenous and European blood. I would have gone further in your case and guessed that your Hans Taaibosch might conceivably have been someone of Hottentot descent. But I did not realize that you had ever been to South Africa. Perhaps you could tell me where you met him there and I could perhaps place him more accurately.'

My eyes had become accustomed to the dark and so bright was the starlight that I could see the outline of her head above the driving wheel as she shook it and, in a tone grey with a disappointment beyond my understanding which the answer produced in her, she replied flatly, 'I've never been to South Africa. I cannot help you in that regard much as I would like to, because it is so important to me to know as much as I possibly can about him now.'

She paused and although I noticed the emphasis on the now and was perturbed by its vehemence, I for my part remained silent because there was nothing for me to add and I had no hunch of any kind to tell me what she was really after until she remarked, as if some hope had revived in her, 'You say he might conceivably have been of Hottentot descent and you did say in the course of your talks at Pendle Hill that the praying mantis was also known in Africa as the Hottentots' god. Could the Hottentots have been the same therefore as the Bushmen?'

'I'm afraid not,' I told her. 'They had certain things in common but they were totally different people.'

'How and why?' she asked curtly, as if in haste to know.

I explained why at some length and with great care, more than ever convinced that it mattered more to her than I could possibly know. At the end of it, far from being discouraged, she announced, hitting the wheel with her left hand for emphasis, 'The more you tell me the more I'm certain he was one of them. Somewhere, some time he was one of them. And I'll tell you something. Ever since you started talking to us about these people and their stories, I've felt as if you were telling me something about Hans Taaibosch that, in order to understand him properly and appreciate him for the miracle he was, I should have known but never knew. I felt almost as if you had come specially to us on his account, and I was there to hear and listen to what you had to say as his intermediary, as if in some way to bring you together. I know it makes no sense at all but I feel this more strongly now in spite of the fact that all you've told me seems to argue against it. He must be, he's just got to be one of them. Is it truly impossible for a real Bushman to have had a name like Hans Taaibosch?'

'No of course not,' I told her, again feeling almost criminal that I should have to go on and qualify the statement. 'But branded with a name like that, the chances are that he could not have been a true Bushman and was either of mixed European and Bushman origin or at least so uprooted that he must have ceased utterly to be representative.'

'But I promise you,' she answered vehemently, almost indignantly. 'There was no sign of European blood in his appearance. He looked exactly like the Bushmen of the desert as you described them to us. He must have been one of them, although terribly uprooted as you say, or I couldn't have met him as I did.'

'Where did you meet him then?' I asked.

'Why, here in New York. I thought that was obvious all along.'

It might have been obvious to her, but nothing could have been less obvious or indeed more improbable to me. The great Delaware river was already well behind us. We had crossed it not far from where George Washington had made his own historic crossing some two hundred years before and as our crossing had been by ferry low on the water we had been put into a state of great intimacy with the black river flowing so broad and yet so deep and urgently into the night. Out of this intimacy and the fact that it was midnight came a sense as of participation in the ritual progression of a dream, and a feeling of having passed not only a physical frontier but a border of space and time where reality was extended, so that

47

anything true that had ever been could be overtaken and recovered, until there came a re-awakening as if by alarm clock when I noticed how high already the silhouette of New York was drawn across the sky ahead. I watched one tall pinnacle of light after the other rise to illuminate the dark ahead like a display of fireworks, obsessed more than ever with the incongruity of what my companion was inflicting on me and its grave implications of the capriciousness of chance, for which I have so much inborn reverence, reckless enough to have brought about a meeting between the civilized and sophisticated person at my side and a Bushman in such a city, when hardly any of my own countrymen had ever had a chance of even seeing one.

The last thing I wanted to do however was to diminish any meaning that her acquaintance with this mysterious Hans Taaibosch held for her by dwelling on the improbabilities inherent in all I had heard. I felt that the least I could do was to suggest, I hoped helpfully, 'Well that could be easily settled. All you have to do is to bring us together and I'm certain I could tell you precisely what he is in a few seconds.'

'I'm afraid that's not possible now,' she said with a tone that was heart-rending. I just could not ask her why it was not possible, but felt I had to wait until she was ready to tell me.

'But surely you must have asked him yourself?' I said, after some inner deliberation with myself.

'I'm afraid I did not. He seemed so much one of us by the time I met him. In any case, I had never heard of either Bushman or Hottentot until you spoke about them to us. I didn't know enough to ask any real questions. That's the hell of it, you see. He must have had so much to tell us if only we had known enough to solicit it and to understand how to receive what he would have had to tell. But he always appeared so happy that one didn't suspect there could be anything important lacking in his life. Oh, how unimaginative can one be! And now of course it's too late.'

She was silent for a long while. The city's outline quickly rose higher and its intrusion into the sky ultimately became so arrogant that the evocation of midnight heavy with its load of stars was torn from us, the archaic moment of belonging and meaningful transition produced at the ford of the urgent river lost in the dark behind us, and a kind of artificial, contrived rhinestone present took over completely in front.

Happily she was more used to it than I and in that regard at least could not have been at all put out, for she was the first to break the silence and say, brighter than at any moment during the journey, 'But I have something I could show you that might help you to tell me exactly what he was. Please let me bring it to you tomorrow. Any, any time you say.'

I could not say no to someone so hurt and eager and in any case by now there seemed no other choice left. Indeed I have never felt less of a chooser at any time since Martha Jaeger had first sent me the news that mantis had appeared in a dream in America. On the contrary, I felt chosen, why and for what was not yet clear, knowing only that the difficulty of being chosen is that the choice has already been made, all questions of personal alternatives eliminated and no option left except one of surrender to whatsoever, out of all the infinite number of possibilities open to chance and circumstances, has so mysteriously picked on oneself.

It was to be my last crowded two days in America and I had to end them by going to a farewell gathering at

A Mantis Carol

Martha Jaeger's on the last evening. But since this lady was invited too, I suggested that we should go afterwards to the apartment lent to me by my publishers in Park Avenue South and look deeper into this matter of Hans Taaibosch's identity.

There seemed nothing else to say for the moment so I was prepared to hold my peace and wait until then. But I am certain we must have talked more because the journey to my apartment lasted another half an hour or so. Yet I have no recollection of anything of consequence passing between us, so central to all my thinking had this issue of Hans Taaibosch become. But what I do remember was that as we drove up Fifth Avenue and past Central Park on my way, all along the route was graced with Christmas trees. The trees were not bright so much as glowing with electric light, each spire of green lit in a manner that, for the first time I think endeared this artificial light to me and made it so at home to eyes born to lamp and candle, that I was able to recover the feeling of the midnight sky and its spread of stars above the archaic ford, and in this profound reassociation found it all in the authentic line of succession to the night, which the shepherds declared silent and still as it was holy and of which we sang at just this time of the year when I myself was young in Africa.

MANTIS FOLLOWS THROUGH

Mantis Follows Through

I HAD so much to do during the day which followed that we returned to my apartment from Martha Jaeger's farewell party late at night, my packing still undone and I myself due to leave for England early in the morning if I were to be back home in time for Christmas. Also I was tired, not only physically but of people and their endless questions and demands during the exacting weeks behind me. The pull between my own necessities and the need for being both patient and solicitous with this woman despite my curiosity, accordingly created tensions within me that were almost unbearable.

Quickly I helped her off with her coat and saw her into a comfortable chair. I drew the curtains so that the late-night traffic rushing by towards the old Grand Central Station and beyond was audible only as some kind of trade wind of time bringing up the ship of the stripped earth over the horizon of its swollen water.

Indeed it was so still in this large, comfortable apartment that I could hear the large refrigerator in the kitchen switch itself on and its motor vibrating as if it were the engine responsible for the dynamics of this mystery of meaning about to be delivered at that late hour in that deep, cushioned room.

I sat down near her and waited with impatience, I fear ill-concealed, for her to show me whatever it was she had

brought. It was, I assumed from the large cardboard fold-
ers tied in a red ribbon which she propped up against
the side of her chair, a drawing, painting or blown-up
photograph of some kind. Yet she seemed to be in no
hurry to let me see it. Instead she tried to lead me into
a discussion about the party and people who had been
there. I was on the verge of outright rebellion against the
irrelevance of it all and telling her sharply to get on with
whatever it was about.

I leant forward to interrupt and saw her face more
clearly. At once the temptation to any show of impatience
vanished because she was so obviously afraid, now that
the moment had come to face a judgement on the last
evidence she had to produce, and which she knew she
would have to accept as final.

I had to entice her into letting me put the folder on
the table between us and it was almost as if I were removing some ornament especially precious to it from the
fist of an inarticulate child, so that I quickly drew back
to leave the folder unopened in front of her. That did it
however, for she leant forward and I saw fingers trembling as she undid the ribbon. Even so she hesitated again
before she turned over a heavy cardboard cover to reveal
something that lay like a shadow within a large sheet of
white tissue paper. Again she faltered and I was tempted
to lean forward, pick up the paper myself and whip it
aside.

Yet I was restrained by a feeling that it would be a
form of sacrilege to do this to a woman who had nursed
whatever it was so delicately, secretly and reverently for
so long. The mystery was her child and if it were ever to
be undressed and be naked and unashamed between us
her hand alone had the right to do it.

But I remained silent and helpless, until suddenly she

looked up and her grey eyes, dark with apprehension, exclaimed, 'It must look silly to you but now that the moment's come, I'm afraid to show it to you. Showing it might be the end of something that has been very dear to me even if it were true to me only as a fantasy.'

I tried to reassure her. I said something banal to the effect that nothing could ever destroy the reality of fantasy that came truly from the heart as hers appeared to me to have done. Whatever the truth it would only promote and not diminish the purpose of the reality her fantasy had served.

'Do you really think so?' she asked, somewhat rhetorically because my words already seemed to have reassured her enough to take up the tissue paper delicately by the corner and draw it smoothly aside.

I found myself looking down at the photograph of the head of a man, cast in bronze. It was not necessary to take it up and hold it closer to the light. Whoever had sculpted it was a person of exceptional gift because the head had been beautifully modelled with the inevitability of an absolute compulsion of imagination. In the light of the lamp on the table the face came out three-dimensionally so clearly that it was more vivid, alive and conclusive than I believed any photograph or painting could have been.

Also the head had been photographed in some panchromatic tone very close to the original native apricot brown of the subject, since one glance had been enough to satisfy me that I was looking at the face and head of one of the truest of true Bushmen.

The conviction was total and the long-term effect of the woman's hopes and anxieties on me by now so great, that I had an impulse to shout out an answer which would banish doubt from her for ever. Even so, speaking with

as measured a voice as I could, my words sounded unnaturally loud in my ears, 'Hans Taaibosch, I presume.'

Uttering the word 'presume' I felt like some kind of
latter-day Stanley who had been charged by a deep unexplained anxiety, and sense of loss of the age in which he
lived, to find what had become of a Stone-Age Living-
stone long vanished and apparently imperilled if not per-
ished in exploring the heart of darkest New York. So
great was this conviction of having found someone of her
as well as my own unconscious expectation that it was
surprising that I did not hold my hand out to the photograph as well.

She did not say yes or no, I expect because by now she
was fixed only on what was essential. She clenched her
hands tightly and asked in a voice taut with haste, 'But
is he please, *is* he or *isn't* he?'

There was no need to ask what the is or isn't referred
to, and I hastened to announce, amazed at the power of
the joy I felt in being able to do so, 'Yes of course he is!
He is the purest of pure Bushmen you could possibly
ever meet.'

'Dear God,' she exclaimed, hardly believing yet that
she could have been right after all, and both overawed
and humbled by the realization.

She sat back in her chair to hold her head in her hands
and shudder with whatever the human heart feels when
its most secret, lonely and improbable intuitions nursed
against all the odds of time, circumstance and place are
at last vindicated.

It is a place in the human spirit where I myself have
occasionally stood in other ways and I knew how necessary silence and reverence were for nursing the gratitude induced in one by such an act of generosity from
life itself towards the so slight, improbable and vulnerable

56

promptings of our hearts, and I could only contribute to the moment, despite the unexplained incongruity and improbability of it all, still coming at me from the image of Hans Taaibosch lying there on the table at that time in such a city, by repeating as if the words were a lullaby putting fear finally to sleep. 'Yes, it's a Bushman head, a beautiful Bushman head. Look at the wide, high cheekbones, the Mongolian slant of eye, the pointed Pan-like ears, the oval face, the fine-drawn chin, the unique peppercorn head of hair. There's no doubt that it is a Bushman head of the purest classical features conceivable. But what on earth could he have been doing in New York, and who moulded and shaped him so well and . . . '

The questions came rushing out so fast now that she had taken her hands from her head and was sitting up looking at me with clear untroubled eyes.

However, she interrupted me not to answer any of my questions but to add to what I had been saying, 'You should have seen him in person and you would have recognized the little body, beautifully made as you described it to us, the feet, neat and small, narrow ankles and a behind that protruded as much as a stomach sticking out in front, all so rounded and prominent as you said they did in a good season in the desert and I'm glad to say that from the time I knew him in New York it was always a good season for him.'

For the first time her tone was light and there was a smile on her face at this recollection of Hans Taaibosch's chid-man shape so that she could refer almost gaily to one of the many things I had told her about the Bushmen; how his body had features found in no other human body on earth, like this behind for instance. It enabled him to store nourishment there in a good season for leaner days to come. It was to the economy of his body what a hump

57

is to that of a camel or kudu, or for that matter the 'Ngoni cattle of the Zulus, and their fat-tail to the sheep of the Hottentots. It was the biological seal of authenticity Africa put on all that was peculiarly its own and was its way of arming its children against long years of deprivation and drought, giving either humps, tails or behinds to the bodies as places for storing up nourishment which no other human species possessed. I had told them all, of course, how I myself had seen in a good season of rain and food in the desert the behinds of Bushmen growing enormously and in a lean season shrink until they looked like any normal human behind and she had obviously derived great support against doubt in the past by recalling that fact, as was obvious from her change of tone.

'Yes,' she said, with unexpected cheerfulness. 'I'm not suggesting that he was ever so over-fed that he resembled the one Bushman you told us about whose behind was so prominent that a bottle of brandy and two glasses could be stood on it, but he did have to be taken to a special tailor. There was never anything in the shops that fitted him straight away. Always the trousers, coat and waistcoat had to be carefully measured and cut to fit that remarkable little figure. And . . . '

Her voice faltered, no doubt because she was seeing him in a visual idiom of her own for which no words, however precise could be a substitute. I wished I could have followed her there and seen him standing as clearly before me in this room, so that the last of the turbulence from the storm of astonishment within me caused by the incongruity of his presence in New York, so far from his natural home, could be left behind and removed for good the objections of reason and logic against the interference which his presence on such a scene constituted for a masculine sense of the importance of law and order in the human scene of things.

'And then there was his laughter.' I heard her take up the verbal thread again. 'I wish you could have heard him because that too was so like the Bushman laughter you told us about. It was quite irresistible. It was just enough to hear him laughing and one was compelled straight away to join in without knowing the cause. When you told us that you would have given anything you possessed in the world to be able to laugh like that, you were only saying what I often felt when I was with him.'

Of all the many things she had said up to then, perhaps that churned me up most. The thought that such a child of the desert as he now appeared to have been could have gone on laughing even in this skyscraper world had a staggering import for me. They all pointed to one overwhelming fact — the existence in him of a kind of bond with life so characteristic of the Bushman and so strong that nothing, even exile in the last extremities of what was totally the unimagined and unimaginable for him, could erode it. And I wondered whether had I heard such laughter in such a place I would have been able to enjoy it as this woman had obviously done and not have been perhaps a little afraid instead and even overcome by it, as if it invoked a comparison with our own palid gift of laughter so odious as to become a fearful warning of how fast the tide of life, instinctive and immediate, had receded within us.

This and so many more unfamiliar feelings and reactions crowding in on me, suggested that the time had come for us to get down to what passes for facts today, putting first things first and begin at the beginning, if I were ever to get to know Hans Taaibosch himself and be enabled to make my peace with his appearance in this improbable place.

'Don't you think you ought to tell me before you go on how he came to be here, what his life was, what he did here and how you came to meet him, and everything you can recall about him; all the details down to the identity of the sculptor who made this head?'

She began with the last of my questions and announced rather shyly that she had done the head herself and that if there was any merit in the portrait it was because he had been so good a sitter. He had enjoyed being done more than anyone she had ever sculpted. He had loved every moment of it, she said, and had made her feel somehow that it was the most important thing she had ever done, so uniquely did he convey to her how much it all mattered to him.

For instance, he was always getting off his chair to stand beside her. Every time he noticed how like his own likeness the clay was growing under her hands, he would do an expressive little dance of acknowledgement for her, before bounding gaily back to his chair.

Above all there was the moment when she had done her work on his head as well as she could, and, despite an intense dissatisfaction at what was still left out, could use those words that, for an artist conscious of all the other possibilities and subtleties of interpretation and expression shut out in the finality of any given form, are as much a sentence of death as a certificate of birth: 'I have finished.'

He had jumped excitedly from his chair and come to stand beside her, unusually silent and still, looking at the clay model of his face and head. He stood there for so long without a word that she thought him disappointed. But suddenly he almost shouted, 'You, Hans Taaibosch,

you child of . . . ' She could not tell what he was a child
of because the word was uttered with a series of clicking
consonants, the like of which she had never heard again
until I spoke to them at Pendle Hill.

'It must have been "child of a Bushman", I'm sure,
with "Bushman" in his own tongue,' I interposed.

She seemed glad of that and her words followed on
unimpeded. 'He suddenly shouted then, as you suggest,
"you child of a Bushman, you. What are you doing there
with my face but without my body?"

'He then laughed a deep, low laugh of content from
the pit of his stomach. Then, solemn as I have never
known him, he put his hand on my shoulder, to ask, "Did
you really do all that just for old Hans Taaibosch — just
for him?"

'I said, why yes, of course. And do you know, he sat
down on my studio floor, wept for the one and only time
I've ever seen him weep and then, just as suddenly, he
stopped, jumped up and did a dance all round the studio
that shook the furniture as I was already shaken within.
It was the loveliest dance I have ever seen and it was I
and not he who ended up in tears.'

'I'm not surprised,' I said. 'They would always rather
dance out their deepest gratitude than put it into words.
It is the loveliest of all their dances. They do it for the
animals they've killed for food to thank them for allowing
themselves to be killed so that they can live. And I never
see their dancing without feeling deeply moved and utterly irreverent and blasphemous because of our own
incapacity for acknowledging what life will give if only
we will let it.'

She seemed grateful for the elaboration because she
put her own hand briefly, shyly on mine before saying,
'But the strangest thing of all was that from that day on,

61

A Mantis Carol

I believe he was happier than ever, and somehow more confident, almost as if he had added inches to his height.'

'You see how much you gave,' I could not help an 'I-told-you-so' note to my voice because it might be able to silence this strong self-reproach she seemed to suffer on behalf of Hans Taaibosch.

I thought it so important by now that she should be convinced of this that I went on to elaborate and say how I believed that she had given him something which none of us can ultimately do without, an 'act of recognition' of his own individual dignity in life. I thought no one could do it as well as an artist, because the artist, by making us part of his own process of creation which is involved in the continuing deed and act of universal creation from which we have become estranged as Hans Taaibosch must have been before, restores us to our own sense of belonging and makes us feel known and at home in life again.

I believed that what she had made in what appeared a mere portrait to her was a mirror reflecting a universal authenticity made specific in him. I emphasized why I thought he was not unique in this in order to bring out the significance of what I felt she had done. None of us, however assured and permanent our systems appeared to be, I suggested, could ever know our own full selves unless we had some positive act of recognition by something other than ourselves. But our systems could not be less assured and more confused and our own especial allotment of universality tended to be lost in the dim and blurred reflection of all individuality in the great, grey impersonal collect of our time, massing like some Gothic horde to overwhelm the spirit of specific man.

No matter how urgent our hearts, we all needed at least another to make us the one we were meant to be.

Mantis Follows Through

The mystery of our deepest self, the mystery of all things, indeed the mystery of creation itself was always between two; in an awareness that there are always both a 'thou' and an 'I'. Many of us today were condemned to experience the 'I' and the 'thou' solitarily and darkly only within ourselves unconfirmed by the world about us. Most of us indeed had become distorted into knowing only the 'I' of themselves and not the 'thou'. But in so far as we could experience them we did so alone because the mirror of our time was cracked, and indeed for Hans Taaibosch must have been utterly shattered, until on the day she declared that the clay still warm between her fingers was fulfilled, and at last he was able to look and see the kind of reflection of his own living worth which I had mentioned. She must please accept how lucky he was that his 'thou' within had found also a 'thou' without, to reflect it for him.

'You were such a "thou" to him,' I repeated, almost begging her to accept the statement. 'So are you surprised and not a little ungrateful to go on questioning what you have done yourself?'

HANS TAAIBOSCH AT HOME

Hans Taaibosch at Home

SHE thanked me gravely and solemnly as a child before going on to say that there were no end of personal
impressions like those she could describe to me, but
added apologetically that there were very few facts that
she could produce at first hand herself. She felt singularly
guilty about that part of it now, but the trouble was that,
by the time she came as a child to know Hans Taaibosch,
he appeared so much part of the scene that he might
have belonged to it always, and it never occurred to her
to look before and after his coming into their life. She
knew vaguely that he had been born in Africa. But, as
far as she and her friends were concerned, the story had
its beginning in Jamaica about halfway through the First
World War and that, too, she only knew at second hand.
She herself had not even been born then and only knew
what she had heard from the family of the American
lawyer who adopted him and in whose home she had
met him. Yes, it was a lawyer who acted for a great
American circus who had first met Hans Taaibosch when
on holiday in Jamaica.

One sultry evening he went to a variety show in a rather
shabby Kingston theatre and there suddenly was Hans
in the limelight, naked except for a sort of skin bikini,
dancing and prancing and displaying his remarkable little
figure for the delight of a bored, well-nourished and well-

wined audience. Although he was the great success of the evening and the audience laughed at his dancing and his shape as if they were the funniest things they had ever seen, the lawyer, an unusually imaginative and sensitive person, was repelled by something in the quality of the laughter.

She remembered him saying that it was so arrogant and contemptuous as if Hans Taaibosch were there merely to confirm by contrast how well and how much better life had made their own breed. He was even more repelled when, despite Hans Taaibosch's dynamic performance and a plausible appearance of loving every minute of what he was doing, he thought he discovered a profoundly forlorn, sad, rejected, even humiliated little person at the core of it all. It was somehow more than he could take and his New England conscience compelled him to go round to the dressing-rooms after the show. He was lucky enough to find Hans Taaibosch alone and had him to himself long enough to confirm in a strange kind of English that he was most unhappy and in a plight from which he longed to be delivered but had long since despaired of ever escaping.

They got no further when the man who claimed to be his promoter appeared. He was a large, red-faced, beery, moustached Englishman who professed to be a captain in the British army, a profession which to a lawyer's quick analytical mind seemed immediately open to doubt, for what could a captain in His Majesty's forces be doing playing at theatricals in Jamaica when his country was engaged in the greatest and most desperate of wars in Europe? From his behaviour and manner the lawyer concluded that if the man confronting him had been in the British army at all it could at the most have been in a much humbler capacity.

But all that was academic at the moment. Whether captain, non-commissioned officer, or other rank, there on British territory he had a standing which an American lawyer did not. Hans Taaibosch was in the man's power as firmly as any slave of a slave-owner in the days when slavery was both legal and respectable. Enquiries he made the next day confirmed this and yet the impression made on him by Hans Taaibosch, particularly his feeling as of some rare being caught in a trap, stayed with him so forcibly that he became determined to know more and somehow to try to help him.

For an instant she broke off her narrative that I was finding more and more engrossing, to explain what was obviously crucial to her. 'You see, it was not only me Hans affected so. He had the same effect on this lawyer who knew the world and men — and, good, sensitive and imaginative a man as he was to the end of his days, he must have been disillusioned by people often enough in his work not to be unduly impressionable and naive about them. Yet there in a climate which he told me he detested because it made him feel so uncomfortable that he never went back, he reacted with the utmost vigour and did something completely out of character.'

She told me how he set about helping Hans Taaibosch in the craftiest of ways. He first set himself to hide his dislike of Hans's promoter and saw to it that he spent as much time as possible in their company. He discovered that years before, she could not remember how many, the so-called captain had somehow got Hans Taaibosch to accompany him out of Africa, and travel the world with him, making a living out of exhibiting Hans as a figure of entertainment, or fun as she preferred to call it.

Since Hans could not read or write, there was no formal written contract drawn up between him and his promoter. The captain's power over him came entirely from the fact that Hans had nobody else to whom he could turn for protection. With an idiom of being and spirit as strange, incomprehensible and different from the contemporary world as the biological idiom in which his own little body had been conceived was from that of other men, any protection was better than none.

Even if the lawyer had a clear plan as to what he could do for Hans which he did not at that moment, it would be impossible on British territory to get him away legally from another British subject like the 'captain', let alone overcome the difficulties he would have to face bringing in to America a person like Hans without passport or visa of his own. Almost at his wits' end, he hit on a plan. If he could persuade the captain that he would have a far better commercial prospect by getting himself and Hans attached to the American circus whose legal representative he was, half his battle would be won. Once he had the two of them on American soil he would be in a greatly more powerful position to act. He could get to know Hans Taaibosch and the captain properly, find out precisely what Hans needed most and what the captain's credentials were and from there work more hopefully towards a solution. The plan worked. Early in 1917 Hans Taaibosch and the captain were travelling the circuits of America as members of the circus for which the lawyer acted.

I do not know much about circuses myself but from what she told me that night and from what I know now as a result of a correspondence I have had with one of the last survivors of the owners of the circus, it must have been an unusually happy, humane and harmonious concern. Hans Taaibosch was immediately at home in it.

Without exception he affected everybody as he had

affected the lawyer. Everyone took him to their hearts and he was, and remained until he was too old to do his piece any longer, without an enemy in its ranks. All were his friends from the owners to the men who pitched the great top and the people who performed within the magic ring. The lion tamers, who came and went, not unnaturally were immediate objects of his admiration but on the whole the clowns mattered most to his own warm and spontaneous heart as if in their tumbling, constant humiliation and incorrigible capacity for laughing at their misfortunes, he saw his own unrecorded fate portrayed, and thus felt accompanied, needed, wanted and so became content. But not so the captain.

From the start he was out of his depth in such company and so unprofessional and alien in his own egotistical approach to circus life that within a year or two he had vanished from the scene. She did not know the final why and how of it. All she knew was that the lawyer and the owners of the circus had contrived it so that Hans was left behind, free to pursue a career of his own, and the captain gone for good. From then on Hans spent all the summer months travelling the wide circus beat of America. There was nothing that she had ever heard to indicate that he was anything but extremely content in doing this. The lawyer looked after his money for him so that he was always independent and in the fall, when the circus tours ended and the great tents folded, he returned to New York to be welcomed as a child of the family in the home of the man who had liberated him.

Of that period of Hans Taaibosch's life she could speak with more knowledge and greater personal authority. She could vouch for the fact that he was in a sense the life of the household. He had a particular gift with children. There was not a child who entered the family who did

71

not instantly become his friend; something she thought that I would especially understand, because had I not spoken to them at Pendle Hill with such love of my own Bushman nurse and the two little old Bushman friends I had as a child myself on my grandfather's farm in Africa?

However alien life in such a household must have been to him as she now realized and however good and comfortable in the final analysis it could not have been a pattern he would ideally have sought for himself. Yet he showed no signs of it not being sufficient. If only he had not looked so happy, perhaps she might have been tempted to look deeper and ask the sort of questions that would have produced the answers to enable her to be a companion to what she was now certain after what I had told them must have been a singularly lonely and deeply exiled part of himself.

She said this with such evident distress again that I felt bound to try and comfort her by gently reprimanding that part of herself that was in rebellion, as if it were an uncomprehending child and said, 'It's an excellent thing, that New England conscience you've mentioned, and which this wonderful lawyer followed so imaginatively — and of which you obviously have your full measure. But you mustn't carry it too far. From what you have told me, it's clear that you all gave him all you had of trust and affection, and you must surely accept that as having been companion enough, and certainly something that he could never have experienced in a similar degree anywhere else before.'

'No, no,' she said emphatically, making a fist of her right hand and hitting the cushioned arm of her chair. 'You're saying something which you yourself could not possibly believe. What about that Bushman convict you told us of who had found a family to house and love him

in Africa and yet spoke those heart-rending words to his
benefactors of how he was waiting for the moon to "turn
back" so he too could whisk about on his own heels and
return to the place he had come from because it was the
time when his people would be telling one another the
kind of stories that he longed to hear. Remember how
you told us that, even more than being homesick for a
place of his own and people he knew, he was homesick
for a story of his own and what sort of a story could he,
Hans Taaibosch, have found in a place like this?'

And she waved her hand at the windows behind us as
if she expected them to be wide open to reveal the alien
outline of the lofty city and its streets filled with the
mechanical traffic of a contrived and, in Hans Taaibosch's terms, unnatural life. 'Surely, you of all people
must know how he must have missed his own story and
a thousand and one things besides in a place like this?'

I felt rebuked and yet not invalidated, and came back
to urge, 'Yes, I am certain all that is true, but you gave
the best of what you could give and that always gets
through and in the end must be and is enough. I promise
you all that is true. I say it not only as someone who
knows something of Bushmen but I know this desperate
world of ours, and in that regard I am overcome by Hans
Taaibosch's good fortune in having been put by life in
the path of someone so good as your lawyer, to work in
so unusual a circus as you have described and having a
friend like yourself and not vanished, unwanted and persecuted, into the anonymous dust of history as his people
have done for so many and such terrible millennia. I can't
tell you what it does for me. It moves me to tears. And
if it does that to me, imagine what more it must have
done to Hans Taaibosch, coming as it did to him when
he must have been close to a final despair. Except of

course that his kind never despaired, or there would not be any of them left today, few as they are.'

She made a face as if what I had just said, even at such length, was not enough to comfort her — but did not protest any more. She went on to say how, judging by what she knew now, Hans made their life and their stories a proxy for his own out of this capacity of the Bushmen for participating in all that surrounded them which I had described in my talks to them as almost mystical. He had a gift which was truly remarkable that enabled him, without surrender of his own hidden and uncomprehended identity, to enter into the spirit of whatever they happened to be doing and even partake of the character of the people who came and went in and out of the house as if it were food for his own.

It was not just that he appeared to know what the people were like within their own hidden selves but could actually become them. I knew now as well as she did how unlike any Americans that had ever been, her Hans must have been in spirit and appearance. Yet she had seen lawyers, artists, businessmen, scientists and priests walk out of the house after only their first meeting with Hans Taaibosch and he would give an imitation of each one of that motley band so true and revealing that they were helpless with laughter. It was even more than an imitation. It was extraordinary how, as one watched that unique little Bushman shape in its preposterous American dress, he would suddenly cease to be himself and become translated into some lawyer, doctor, artist or priest to such an extent that he was more like any of them than they themselves were.

I recognized the gift from my own experience of Bushmen and could have confirmed her reading of Hans Taaibosch's capacity a hundredfold but did not want to impede this advance of her recollection of the man which was bringing me so close to him that at any minute I would not have been surprised to see the head on the table joined by its three-dimensional body and Hans Taaibosch arise and come to sit down as a person of flesh and blood in the vacant chair beside us.

I was more than grateful for my own restraint since she went on to add perhaps the most valuable nuance of all for me.

She explained that in all this imitation there was no hint of caricature. It was utterly without malice or mockery and full only of implications of the purest of concerns for what the imitated persons quintessentially were. The laughter provoked was not directed *at* the imitated persons so much as with them, because of their release from a kind of human bondage. It was full of a vicarious happiness over such an act of emancipation of personality from the pretensions, preconceptions and other frustrations of custom and conformity in which Hans Taaibosch's audience were as much encaged as those he had imitated.

And what went on within the household among all who entered it applied also to the life of the great America without. Whatever Hans did in the circus, exposed to the glare of the limelight within the sawdust of the great ring and the laughter from tier upon tier of foreign white faces, was, she was certain, so successful because the same kind of quality emerged from whatever he did. She was certain because in a sense the macrocosmic part of his life in America was clearly refocused in the microcosm of the home. She said she was certain with confidence now, but she had to confess that in the beginning she had found the experience of seeing him at the centre of public circus laughter over-painful to her and, had it not been for Hans

Taaibosch himself, she would never have returned to see
him perform after her first experience of it.

But that was not the immediate point. What mattered
was that whatever interested the lawyer and his family
and friends interested Hans. At the time she thought it
was because it held the same kind of interest for him as
it did for them all, but she realized that his interest came
out of a respect and love for them and was based on the
assumption that even what he himself could not understand must be intrinsically important because it was important to them. As he could not read or write, his interest
in the outer context of his life in America could never be
intellectualized or framed as ideas or mental conceptions.
He could only know them through an act of participation
in the life of the household with that profound inbuilt
capacity for doing so which the examples she had already
given she hoped had demonstrated clearly.

From her own experience, she could confirm that there
was nothing, literally nothing which interested them,
however eccentric or even alien, that ultimately did not
interest him as much, innocent and child-like through it
all as if no commitment of judgement or evaluation of
their interest were ever called for from him but all could
be entirely taken for granted as being of ultimate worth.

For instance, as the years went by, he took an increasingly lively interest in American politics. She was certain
that he must have understood their politics even less than
she did and he undoubtedly had none of the reservations
that she had about its character and value, but just because the lawyer and his children and their friends took
it seriously, Hans Taaibosch became almost a fanatic in
his conversion to their political concerns.

Local, state and Federal politics, all aroused a passionate feeling of involvement on his part. He could not read

the newspapers, of course, and had to rely on a process of question and answer for satisfying his interest, but he got to the point where he realized that the most important subjects in the newspapers had the largest, thickest and blackest headlines and during a political campaign, particularly a presidential campaign, he would be the first to snatch the newspaper from the door and, pointing to the largest banner headlines, ask someone to read out meticulously all that was written.

He would work himself up into a kind of fever on the final eve of presidential elections until he trembled all over his body with excitement for hours, like an electric bell ringing at a door which refused to be opened although the caller knew people were within. When the result was announced his elation, if it was in accord with the political allegiance of the lawyer's family, was pitched much higher than their own. If not, his despair turned the morning black in the brightest of breakfast rooms.

'Just look here,' she commanded as she lifted up the large photograph of Hans Taaibosch to reveal a pile of snapshots underneath and picking the one at the top held it out to me, 'Here is a photograph of Hans taken the morning after Calvin Coolidge's election.'

I took the photograph from her and held it up to the light and there I saw Hans Taaibosch for the first time with his head joined to his body.

He was wrapped in a smart dressing-gown, sitting back deep in the same kind of chair as the ones we were sitting in and the New York *Herald Tribune* wide open on his knees. He was pointing at a large headline announcing in the journalese of the day that there had been a famous presidential victory. But even more startling to me than this evidence of how a representative of the first people of my own native country, born to the last of what was

77

left of a Stone-Age culture, could be overwhelmingly interested in an American presidential return, was the expression of utter resolution and unmistakable happiness on those authentic Bushman features.

The expression was so convincing that for the first time I readily understood why no one had been provoked to be more curious about the life which had preceded that moment. I became so immersed in the repercussions produced within me by all this that I heard her, as though from a great distance, continue to give instances of his identification with the life of America. But perhaps the best thing was to let the pile of snapshots speak for them all.

There were a great number of them spread out fanwise on the cardboard cover. She now produced them for me chronologically and it was extraordinary how the texture and quality of them conveyed Hans Taaibosch's passage through time and gave me a feeling that he was there in the room growing older by the minute, without any suggestion of becoming less happy with the passing years, or of wanting to return to his home in the desert in my own native Africa, from which I was by now absolutely certain he had originally come.

This feeling was stimulated not merely by the fact that he was a little older in each successive photograph but that the cameras with which he had been photographed became more and more modern and the quality brighter so that it was almost as if he were emerging slowly out of a brown blur and haze of a Kalahari dawn behind us towards the electric lit moment in that room, and the technological advance in photography became some sort of time-machine carrying him on into old age and towards his as yet undisclosed end, if end there had been.

The earliest photographs had been taken by Box-Brownie

and showed him as a man already in the second half of his life, but still young enough for the bone to be visible beneath the skin, the dark slanted eyes comparatively unwrinkled at their corners and looking out over the high Mongolian cheeks at me with an untroubled gaze, still full of the wonder of eyes for ever focused on a time when the world was young and all creation still moving through this vision, and fresh with a fierce clarity as if still burning from the touch of the magnetic fingers that had just delivered it from the cold, dark and shapeless clay. It was an expression of eyes which, no matter how experienced and how many times compelled to look on the reiteration of an alien dreary pattern of existence, would until they were extinguished continue to see all as if for the first time.

But always it was that archaic face and expression of the man which impressed one most, so that when one noticed the dress which covered the body one was as resentful as astonished by the clothes. For instance, in one of those faded brownish prints, he stood holding a thick cloth cap in his hand while he wore a coat and waistcoat of the same material — a loud check pattern, a woollen shirt and tie, a pair of full plus-fours complete with appropriate flashes above the calves, legs below hidden in woollen stockings disappearing into a pair of the broguiest of brogues. On the back was written, 'Hans, golf course, Miami, 1922'.

But as the years advanced, the texture of the snapshots changed. They became of an increasingly smarter, glossier, starker, harsher black and white, the lens prying deeper into the privacy of the skin and bone of the man, without any real concern for what was at the core behind them. The face began to wrinkle more, the creases around the eyes to deepen, the lines on the forehead to become

79

more pronounced; only the expression of the eyes re-mained unchanged, however much the light within them appeared to be diminishing.

The settings too varied in a way that was even more startling than the first vision of this Stone-Age plenipo-tentiary on a golf course. There was one of him with what appeared to be a thick woollen night-cap complete with bobble, pulled down over his ears, an even thicker wool-len pullover clinging tightly to his body so that for the first time one noticed how much he protruded in front and how well he stuck out behind. He was wearing thick gloves now and one hand was grasping a pair of skiing sticks. A pair of baggy skiing trousers fell to his fine ankles and his feet were lost in thick boots clamped on to a pair of skis resting on thick, deep snow. Everywhere around him was a vast expanse of a slope of white with the suggestion of tall pine woods smoking at the back. He looked even more serene and if anything happier in this more unlikely setting. On the back was written, 'Hans, Vermont, 1924'.

She must have noticed how sharp my reaction was because as she leant forward to take back this photograph and hand me another, she exclaimed defensively as if the photograph had proclaimed an outrage on its desert subject, 'But he loved the snow! He loved it more than any of us. The first flake would send him off dancing into the snow with delight and he couldn't wait to dig his fingers into it as if he had really discovered the treasure of the world in it.'

I took the next photograph without commenting on how unnecessary any defence was since I needed no convincing. I knew, from my own experience of the rare fall of snow on the high plateau of Africa where I was born, how the substance which is a platitude of winter in Europe and America was of formidable originality bordering on the miraculous under the sun of Africa.

I was free to give all my attention to Hans Taaibosch standing in the centre of yet another glossy snapshot between my fingers. There he was wearing the smartest pair of what we who coveted them ardently in my own youth as a sign of emancipation and avant-gardism called Oxford Bags, a pair of black and white 'correspondent's' shoes, a contrasting short snappy coat and waistcoat above and on his head a wide brimmed velour hat and a briefcase in his hand. On the back was written, 'Hans, Pennsylvania Station, 1925'.

This was followed by another showing him sitting in some sunlit garden of summer smoking a cigar that was almost as long as himself and the delight provoked within him by the prospect of a smoke almost without end shining like a light on his increasingly wrinkled oval little face.

'He loved smoking cigars,' she commented, a note of remembered concern coming into her voice. 'He loved it so much that it was almost the one thing in him of which we disapproved and yet could not seriously try to talk him out of. I've never seen anyone smoke in the unique way he did. He would take a long, deep pull at his cigar and draw the smoke somewhere deep into himself. He would take the cigar from his lips and hold it in his hand — the smoke all vanished — and go on talking with no indication in his manner of having just taken so powerful a swallow of smoke. It was quite uncanny! We knew that any American who had taken so long and strong a pull at the strongest of cigars such as he preferred would have to blow the huge volume of smoke out immediately or he would have coughed and spluttered until the intake of smoke was expelled from his throat before suffocating

81

him. There he would sit, calmly talking away, the picture of total enjoyment, and not a sign of discomfort on his face or other tell-tale indication of unease, until some minutes later one would notice the thinnest and bluest little swirls of smoke appearing at his nostrils, at the corners of his mouth and believe it or not curling beguilingly round his ears. That would last a full minute and be followed by an even longer and stronger pull at the cigar and so on and on until it was finished, and never any indication from Hans except one of total enjoyment while the cigar lasted and a dismay that was comic when it was ended.

'When I was a child there was so much magic in this act for us that whenever he lit up a cigar and started smoking I would have to call the other children in the house and we would all sit round him, wide-eyed and totally absorbed as if he were some wizard and not just another old cigar smoker. I have never ceased to wonder how he managed it. Have you ever seen the like of it yourself?'

I assured her that I had indeed. I knew this was exactly the way the Bushman loved to smoke and had seen them doing it many times. I could tell her how the Bushman already was a smoker of herbs, leaves and even the cannabis he called *dagga* long before the European acquired the habit, and above all how always he smoked as if smoking were something more than an indulgence of a passing taste, a craving for a new physical sensation or just another means of killing time. I said I thought it was always to them also some sort of religious act involved with the repercussions of the coming of fire in the life and spirit of the first man to whom he was within the relativity of time a neighbour.

Fire after all was the first great demonstration of something beyond man prepared to engage itself on his behalf in the battle for life and reality on earth; something utterly beyond the here and now, concerned with his well-being, so that however deep the wonder and great the mystery of it, he felt no longer alone after its coming but as it were accompanied by a power greater than himself. Smoking as a result was to him a first sacrament, a partaking of the divine breath and warmth of a great and living mystery. By bringing fire to his lips and drawing its issue within his deepest physical self, making it part of his own breath of being, he was communing with his intimation of divinity as much as any Christian breaking of the bread and drinking of the wine in simulation of the Last Supper. I believed people like Hans Taaibosch smoking would rediscover some of the feelings of the first man at his first fire and his glimmering awareness of having been singularly blessed in being so delivered from the fear of the darkness and the cold which had hitherto enclosed his uncertain life.

I could have elaborated on this and gone on to say that it was because somewhere deep in the unknown of modern man there was a lingering recollection of those associations between smoking and the first fire which was the real attraction for him in the act of smoking and not a mere addiction of the physical senses to nicotine as the world would like us to believe. But seeing how puzzling my explanation already was even to someone so well disposed as herself, I reminded her of the ritualistic role of smoking in indigenous American history and above all the reference to it in one of my favourites among their many wonderful Negro-spirituals, which celebrated in voices coming straight from the bowels of Negro beings; how when in the valley their Lord spoke, out of his mouth too had come fire and smoke.

I think that made some kind of emotional sense to her at least because she added reflectively, 'That was the trouble with Hans. He was always making one feel that he was something we had forgotten to be; something that we had despised and consequently lost. He was almost a living knot tied in the handkerchief of our minds but the heck of it was that we had forgotten what we had tied it for, if you know what I mean.'

And she tried to laugh as if it were purely a joke and not the cover it was for a whole world of imponderables and incomprehensibilities of associations with this much snapshotted little man on the table between us. On the back of this particular photograph was written, 'Hans, Long Island, 1927'.

And so snapshot after snapshot took us on through the unforgiving years with Hans Taaibosch depicted in all the fashions and attitudes which a typical middle-class American of the period would have had to endure until there came one marked, 'Hans, Colorado, 1937'. I experienced suddenly the full shock that we have when we meet again a close friend whom we have not seen for years and when last seen had still been in what is called the full vigour of life. The photograph showed Hans in the last of his seasons and now an old, old little man, almost too old for what he was portrayed as doing. The snow and the slopes were still there unchanged in the manner which by contrast makes our own remorseless subjection to a law of change which exacts our own removal from the unchanging scene all the harder to bear.

Not surprisingly he was even more thickly clothed than before, a heavy muffler round his throat and a kind of Balaclava contraption on his head as if the cold had at last become a peril and no longer a source of enjoyment to him. And oh! the skis and the sticks were gone and he was sitting, somewhat ignominiously I would have thought, in a child's toboggan. Yet the look on his face was undefeated and undismayed although there was for the first time a hint as of the winter within contracting the expanse of resolution on the expression without.

Last of all there was a photograph of Hans indoors. The camera by now was so efficient and keen that its lens was utterly without mercy and it showed his peppercorn head of hair, so black in the beginning that it had glanced off the photographic plate with the sheen almost as of the black of the patent leather hoof of his beloved mystical eland, now white as the snow on which the previous snapshot had left him. The cheeks were sunk in, the full lips stretched taut and drawn back as if to conform to the hollow where his strong, white teeth had been. In the manner of his race the wrinkles in his skin had multiplied so much that had one not experienced the fact one could never have believed that in their own desert beginning they had been just as smooth as they were full of the colour of a swollen, rounded and just ripened apricot.

He was standing in heavy carpet slippers and wrapped in the thickest of woollen dressing-gowns looking up sideways at someone just out of the picture; someone he obviously loved. His wrinkled, aged face was child-like with endearment and reaching out with all the power of his spirit to the undiminished wonder of still being alive even in so alien a place, for yes, he was laughing so happily that it was almost as if one could hear a far-off murmur of the deep ventriloquist rumble in the stomach which normally followed Bushman laughter of that kind.

Old and loaded with a weight of time and burden of multitudinous experience beyond my knowledge or powers of comprehension, the little figure looked none the

85

A Mantis Carol

less somehow timeless and the laughter depicted there
suggesting what is for me the most lasting, heroic and
triumphant achievement of which a human being is capable. With his own world crumbled and long since vanished in the dust of the years racing away into the void
of unrecorded time behind him, he was without natural
context of his own to contain his end. Yet compelled to
experience it alone and without support of his own kind,
this glossy black and white snapshot of him still as a
laughing warrior, proved none the less how ready almost
to the point of nonchalance he was to end his life not
with a whimper but a bang of joy, implying after the most
terrible of yesterdays that the gift of life no matter how
problematical, painful or exacting was always worth it.

Bitterness, resentment, hatred at the end over what
life has given one, I believe, is defeat; gratitude despite
all, victory. Such a look of gratitude unqualified was on
that face, a gratitude so immediate and obviously taken
as a matter of course by Hans Taaibosch himself, that
the question of evaluating it at all, let alone assessing it
as victory, did not arise for him. The assessment was
mine, and what is more, never having witnessed it directly or indirectly in so great a measure before in another
human being, it now moved me as I have seldom been
moved. And the message that all, all had been worth it,
seemed, despite the impartiality and detachment of the
camera, plain enough for a simpleton to read and hardly
needed the confirmation the woman uttered, her cheeks,
not surprisingly, wet with tears: 'It's strange, it was the
happiest I have ever seen Hans and yet he had just forced
himself out of bed against all our wishes, because he was
a very very sick little old man. It was the last photograph
of him ever taken.'

By this time Hans Taaibosch had become so much alive

86

to me and so much had I been able to fill in from my own knowledge and life with his people in the desert, the quintessentials of what he must have been like before he came into this woman's world, that I felt by now I was the only man in the world who knew him not in part, however dear and brilliant that part was to people like herself, but in something of the fullness with which we all long to be acknowledged and known. As a result I was as upset as she was at this announcement of an impending end to an acquaintance which, however vicariously brought about by this woman's love and concern, already stood firm in my imagination, alchemically transformed into one of the most real relationships I have ever experienced, so that it accompanies me wherever I go like a sunset shadow at my side.

What that strange persistent shadow does to me wherever I am compelled to look at it belongs even more to this moment in which it was born than the traffic and travail of the present. Its place is not in hindsight but there in that electric lit room. It is simply this: I wished it had been possible in the lifetime of Hans Taaibosch or, failing that posthumously, for our own sake even more than his, to have conferred some order of merit on him. Unfortunately life in this hour of disintegration has orders only for honouring men for what they do and for the usefulness of the functions they perform. Indeed there are almost more of these than can be consumed by even the prevailing greed for badges of distinction for working to the rule of an impersonal age, but there is not a single order as yet for honouring men just for what they are within themselves.

And I find myself longing for an order whose investment would be introduced by some citation as this, inevitably heraldic in its language since it issues straight from the ancient unrest of the questing heart of man: 'For valour in the field of life, distinguished conduct in the battle of being and steadfastness in defending its quality and texture against aberration and distortion by the prevailing hatred, malice and envy of our collective time, ensuring thereby an example of how devotion to being for sheer being's sake and pursuing it to its own end, is the true glory of life on earth and the unique source of its renewal and increase of meaning and light in the darkness ahead.'

At the head of the first list of honours in a new year of man would appear: 'Hans Taaibosch, Order of Being, First Class'.

THE GREAT DIVIDE

The Great Divide

BUT to return to the fact of that late hour in the tall, luxurious apartment block and my room so high and yellow with light against the black, I remember how frantic the hurrying traffic sounded then, as if tearing people reluctantly from the illusion of well-being and happiness which their uses and usefulnesses had conferred on them through the artifice of all the highly organized distractions of the great city, because by some unacknowledged instinct they knew only too well the still small voice of reckoning which would be raised from an uncared-for self once they were back alone in bed in the dark, making a cell of their room and a prison of their home.

It all made me feel so remote from that world and so close to this profoundly homeless man who had made a home out of his unutterable homelessness that I would not have been surprised if the woman had taken me by the hand just then to lead me into the room where I was certain now her recollection was already deeply committed as if she were his only kin to the last vigil over Hans Taaibosch and seeing he had some company, however alien, at his end. Although death had not been mentioned once between us since we had met, I knew without a doubt now that physically he must surely be as dead as he had most certainly been alive for me in that room

91

and that the manner of his end was about to be put on record in words for the last time.

Yet if that were so, the woman felt her way towards it characteristically obliquely. Wiping her wet cheeks impulsively with the back of her hand like a little girl she asked me in a voice so low that I could hardly hear the words, 'Do you think that Hans Taaibosch, in all his sweetness of character and capacity for happiness of which I assure you I've given you only a few examples, was an exception among his people?'

I shook my head emphatically and heard myself answer with an angry kind of vehemence, 'He was nothing of the kind. I believe he must have been an exceptional being by any standards but he was certainly not exceptional in this. I've known many, many others of his race who are like him in this regard at least.'

'Why then,' she demanded, her voice firm, her eyes bright with an indignation of her own. 'Why then did people hunt them down and kill them without mercy, or is that just another of those exaggerations and prejudices of history?'

I took great pains to reassure her over this as much for my own as well as her sake because somewhere at the back of my mind a suspicion was stirring that the full meaning of all that had happened since I first received the news of the appearance of mantis in a dream would remain inaccessible without a proper perspective in this matter of the persecution of the Bushman in history.

It was, I told her, one of the great horror stories of all time. How far back it began was impossible to say. All one knew from the archaeological evidence was that it started long before there were witnesses capable of recording it and reporting it to the conscience of man as some corrective to the demonic process of elimination. Indeed it appeared to have started so long ago that even if there had been witnesses to record it, it is doubtful whether the kind of conscience capable of reprimanding the perpetrators of the crime had yet been formed in the general spirit of man, although the victim himself seems significantly never to have been inflicted with any urge to kill others, except in self-defence. The best indication I could give her of the age and scale of this process of elimination was to quote two great archaeologists I had known. They had made a speciality of the study of Bushman culture and art, above all his rock painting, which is the most abundant and inspired form of this prehistoric art the world has ever seen. Both had come to the conclusion that the people who painted the walls of the caves at Lascaux and engraved the rocks of the Iberian Peninsula and the Bushmen in southern Africa, shared a common ancestor, who might well have been the little man of folk-lore and fairy tale who once invested the Mediterranean littoral as well as the whole of Africa.

If that were so, his persecution started there long before the coming of Egyptians, Phoenecians, Carthaginians, Greeks and Romans. Indeed she and I who both dwelt so lovingly on the remarkable child-man shape of Hans Taaibosch and his kind, savouring it for the unique variation on the enigmatic human frame which it was, would surely have no difficulty in appreciating the fact that already there was a description in the hieroglyphic records of the Second Dynasty in Egypt of just such a little man who was both an incorrigible hunter and painter. Somewhere the Greeks too spoke of someone like him having been alive in that region even before Atlantis was

93

lost. Herodotus himself picked up the rumours of his existence and referred to him in his great anthology of the more significant historical gossip of his day.

Yet today there was no trace of him either in the Mediterranean world or in North Africa with perhaps only some rock paintings in the hills of the southern Sahara and the fact that one unique part of the body of his woman is still referred to as the *'tablier Egyptien'*, to remind us that he was ever present there. That surely, I told her, would give her some measure of how long, thorough and on what a vast scale his destruction had been, for Egyptian civilization alone had lasted much longer than our own Western era. But even if one dismissed all that as sheer guesswork and confined oneself to what is historically known and irrefutable, the story was horrible enough. For instance, some three hundred years ago when my ancestors landed at the Cape of Good Hope, he still occupied the largest part of southern Africa, hunting, painting the rocks so that the immense scene was a kind of natural Louvre of this oldest of old master's art; dancing under the moon and telling the stories he loved so much at night by his precise little fire, with the lions in the great wings of darkness of this minute theatre of light, providing an appropriate chorus of fate for catharsis of his telling.

Yet only two hundred years later the black and white invaders of southern Africa had already hunted him down, taken his land from him and exterminated him, so that today only a mere handful of his kind remained in the Kalahari desert of Botswana, South West Africa and southern Angola. Even there, as we were sitting safe in that room, his destruction was continuing in the most insidious of ways, and races who at that very moment were railing against injustice, nationalistic *maladies*

94

imaginaires and clamouring for self-determination at the United Nations Organization, had him in their power absolutely and were ensuring his elimination by a total disregard of his own special needs and his right to a life of his own.

That was one reason why I told his story over and over again. Terrible as his rejection in the past had been, ours was more horrible because we could no longer plead ignorance in the court of life. We knew what we were doing to him. In fact his story was the only cool, objective mirror in southern Africa wherein both black and white could see in their own reflections the common fallible features of the fallible human species, and irrefutable evidence of how both were corrupted by their power over this most vulnerable of all natural men to do the most unnatural things to him. If we could recognize there truly how we had aided and abetted one another in a great crime against humanity, our several, national and racial arrogances and self-righteousnesses could drop from us and history become a reconciling agent between our two destructive selves compelling us to re-examine our values in order to pool what we possess of humanity for a single human end.

So far she had listened to me, compelling herself during this digression to silence with increasing difficulty. I was aware all along of an expression of growing horror and distaste on her face which now exploded, her spirit in arms against the nature of what she had heard.

'But why, why?' she thumped a clenched artist's hand on the arm of the chair. 'You haven't told me a single thing to explain why all this could have been done to people so singularly without harm in them. You told me Hans was no exception. You said you knew numbers of his people with as great a measure of sweetness of character and disposition to friendliness and happiness. Why and how then should so many peoples of so many different racial origins and cultures all have combined to kill him off? Surely it couldn't have been simply a question of corruption by power? There must have been something else about the Bushman to have incited them to persecution on such a scale!'

I thought of all the justifications produced by my own countrymen for their treatment of the Bushmen as I had not only read in history but also heard from the lips of the wisest and best of living men like my own grandfather, old Bantu sages, indunas and chiefs of all kinds. All could be summed up in one phrase with which both black and white always concluded their elaborate and highly rationalized justifications. 'You see we had no option. The Bushmen just refused to be tamed.'

I felt I could best begin by avoiding the labyrinthine details of black and white special pleading and tell her this, so I just said, painfully slowly, for suddenly the recollection had made me infinitely sad, 'Everybody who had anything to do with the Bushmen in the past in my native country, which is the only one I can speak of at first hand, says the reason was that the Bushman refused to be tamed.'

'Tamed?' she exclaimed with a look of utter incomprehension and incredulity. 'Tamed? What an extraordinary expression to use about human beings! You tame wild animals; you don't tame people — or do you do that too in that horrible Africa of yours?'

'I know what you mean of course,' I hastened to appease her outburst before it could take command of her emotions and make impossible the ordered progression of our interchange which I knew was necessary if we were ever to arrive at an understanding that I realized now I needed as much as she. 'In a sense you're right. I think there is a way in which both black and white did regard the Bushman in his natural state as a kind of wild animal. But to do justice even to the unjust, as we are bound to do, I regret, if we are ever to understand this horrible business, by "taming", they meant becoming "civilized" in the sense the term held for them at the time.'

That to begin with made some kind of rough sense to her because she commented not without a certain scorn, 'Well of course it would be very wrong not to recognize that a lot of what we call being "civilized" is not living but mere existence, "tame" to the point of deadliness. I think one of the reasons why Hans made so profound an impression on us all is because he lived in our so-called civilized midst without being either tame or wild, but just alive. Yes, yes, that was it — he was so important to us as children just because he was alive, compared to anybody else we knew. Oh, you've no idea how alive he was! He made us all feel, or at least me, that not the people who adopted him were rich — and indeed they were rich by good middle-class standards — but that *he* was the truly rich person and all the rest of us poor. He in a strange way was the giver and we the takers.

'It applied even to his attitude to money. He would have spent it all as fast as he earned it as if it were water from some inexhaustible fountain, if it hadn't been for his protector. It was he who insisted on saving it for Hans Taaibosch, who would never have accumulated a dollar. Hans would have shared his last dime with us all at any moment. But dear Heaven, he was not 'tame' neither did he need any taming. So how the heck could that ever have been a reason for killing off men like him?'

She was as outraged as ever. Yet intuitively she had

97

come nearer to the heart of the matter as I saw it, and indeed as his persecutors regarded it and judged it sufficient cause for eliminating him. I was about to tell her just this, but before I could speak she herself had second thoughts of her own.

She raised her hands as if in an act of surrender to a need for apology and remarked, 'I'm sorry I called your Africa horrible. On reconsideration and thinking about Hans and all the comparisons he evoked in us children, I realize what specialists we in this country are as well, in taming human beings, particularly children, and educating them out of being their natural selves. We are just every bit as bad as your Africa except that we have at least stopped short of physically exterminating one another.'

I reassured her that much as I loved Africa, the application of the term horrible to it historically was not altogether misplaced. What little we knew of its past hardly bore thinking about except in so far as it was a wonderful testimony of how life could survive and be vivid and worthwhile in spite of the horrors of unnatural men, famine, disease and other insecurities marshalled against it. What did matter was that in calling Hans rich and themselves poor, and referring to his capacity for spending money as fast as he earned it, to live indeed as though obedient to the New Testament exhortation to give no heed to any of his tomorrows, she was perhaps touching on one of the fundamentals of Bushman character and culture, which neither black nor white nor indeed any of his many unknown exterminators in the long, unrecorded past could stomach.

It all went back to a great divide in the human spirit, I tried to explain, I fear rather solemnly, so far away still did the glimmer of understanding splutter on the rim of the area of darkness which had covered so great an area of my mind for so long. It all started, I believed, when not only the life of man but also his spirit were divided against themselves into hunter and husbandman. This division was of such long standing and went so deep that it must have been built into the first genes of human life ever conceived. That is why the story of Esau and Jacob, who also personified this fateful division, portrayed them as having fought one another in their mother's womb for the right to be born first. I was convinced as the Old Testament was that the Esau in us, the hunter, was born first and that the Bushman in history both in his way of life and mould of spirit was the purest model accessible to us of the first man, the man born to be hunter.

And I thought it vital to understand fully what the consequences of life on such a principle were. It meant living in a state of complete trust, dependence and interdependence with nature. Indeed the Bushman committed himself to nature as a fish to the sea and nature, which we thought of as red in tooth and claw, was far kinder to him than any civilization ever was. So committed and involved was his being with nature, for instance, that when the annual rains did not fall and the earth was scorched bare under the sun, his woman went sterile and bore him no children. Moreover, it meant that as a hunter his life was one of constant movement, so that he had to travel light and reduce his possessions to the minimum.

A Bushman, to this day living in the Stone-Age way in the Kalahari, possessed a spear, a bow, a quiverful of poisoned arrows, a leather satchel for the half-dozen or so ostrich egg-shells that were his water flasks, a pair of leather sandals, and one or two of them perhaps a musical instrument; but alas no longer the paint brushes and

99

A Mantis Carol

leather girdle with the little antelope horntips filled with
different colours of pigment that his ancestors would never
have been without. That was all. His woman possessed
even less — a leather shawl for strapping in more ostrich
egg-flasks, a wooden stamping block for making the toughest of desert food edible, her grubbing stick and sandals.
Asked to prepare for a journey of a thousand miles, as I
have done, they would be ready to move in ninety seconds, unafraid and confident that nature and their own
natural wits would provide for them on the way.

I myself whenever I said goodbye to them and wanted
to give them a farewell present had been humiliated over
and over again by the realization that there was nothing
of our rich material civilization I could give them that
would not merely clutter up their lives and make life more
difficult for them. If I could give them anything at all it
had to be in an altogether different dimension, but more
of that later. The important thing was that such a way
of life meant that they had no sense of personal property.
It was not that they lacked individuality. They were the
most individualistic of primitive peoples among the many
I have known, and each man, woman and child seemed
always to stand out vivid, clear-cut and precise in his or
her own experience and right of life. But in some strange
way this individuality was maintained and developed as
it were in the interests of all. They would share all they
possessed. When I gave them a cigarette, one man would
take a puff and instinctively pass it down the line to all
the rest including the smallest child and so back again,
ignoring the fact that the proffered packet had held a
cigarette for each one of them. When I shot game for
food and offered to divide up the meat for them, as I had
done on other expeditions for my black African compan-
ions who expected this of me as the one impartial judge

of their individual needs whom they trusted, the Bushmen would say, 'By all means if you wish, but why do such an unnecessary thing? If one eats, all eat.'

Here I told her I so wished she could have seen them in their hunters' life of constant movement, a flicker of precise apricot flame in the trembling, burning desert furnace scene. And oh, how this freedom of movement impelled their imaginations and became as necessary as food to them. I told her how for example I arrived at a desert outpost once to find a Bushman dying in gaol. He had been caught eating a greater bustard he had killed when starving, and as the bird, proclaimed as royal game, was protected by law, he had been sentenced as a result to a month in prison. Immediately he became ill. A doctor was summoned at once, because that was the pity of it, his prosecutors were not monsters without compassion but just ordinary men convinced that they were doing their duty. The doctor could find nothing wrong with him. All he would say to the doctor was that he could not bear not seeing the sun set any more because of the prison walls. He died that night, I am certain because his spirit had been starved to death by this absence of his daily view of the sun going down in that infinitely mythological way it has in the western desert of southern Africa.

'But Hans!' she exclaimed unbelievingly. 'What of Hans then? How could he endure life in a place like this, shut in skyscrapers, apartment rooms in which you can't even open a window because of air-conditioning, elevators, the lot, except while on vacation in the country. Not only did he not die but he thrived on it all. How and why could he do it and the others not?'

I said I thought we were there in the presence of a great mystery and had to look further for the answer. But surely she could understand now on what a different principle his way of life and those of his people were founded to those of his enemies. While he owned nothing, they who came to replace him, as Jacob had replaced Esau in his mother's and even his God's affections, owned much and had a highly developed sense of property. In fact the difference between him and his enemies could be defined as one of the wisest of men I had ever known, an old Afrikaaner hunter, once described to me the difference between African and European man.

'African man,' he had said, '*is*; European man *has*.' Relatively true as that distinction was in regard to black and white, the comparison was even more just when applied to black African and Bushman. In comparison to the Bushman, the black African was a highly sophisticated man of property. He owned cattle, sheep, goats, hens, dogs and ducks, cultivated the soil and manufactured many things. The Bushman owned nothing, cultivated nothing and manufactured nothing except his hunter's and artist's kit. As a result, when they first met and the Bushman regarded the cattle of the white and black invaders of his land as he did the rest of the animal life of Africa, which he had a natural right to kill for food, a war to death began. Two utterly incomprehensible ways of life had man by the throat and in the end, just as Esau lost out to Jacob, the Bushman lost to black and white in southern Africa.

The story of Esau and Jacob had always been for me one of the most tragic and unresolved stories in the Bible. This story of the Bushman in southern Africa was sadder by far and remained perhaps the most poignant piece of history I knew, because the Bushman had done nothing in the physical world to provoke so terrible a fate. The provocation for what it was consisted in the fact that whatever the outward rationalizations for the killing, he was destroyed not so much for what he did as for what he was.

And there I confessed we entered a level of the spirit so deep and subtle that I could only guess at the explanation. I believed profoundly that this great divide in our spirit was brought about as a means for making man a more meaningful whole than he had been before the division; that the Esau and Jacob separation was brought about so that two essential elements of the human spirit they personified could be reunited at the end of their roads of separate development in a greater way than before. Union of like and like was conformity and not strength but weakness; union of diversity and of opposites was the only real unity and source of strength.

It was significant therefore that although the Jacob principle seemed to have won and to have established those it invested as lords of nature, and the hunter like the Bushman to have vanished from the scene, the struggle between the two elements they personified went on and on in the human soul, seeking the transcendent union, the meaningful reconciliation I mentioned. Yes, I stressed more to myself than to her, the human heart was born a hunter, our blood Bedouin, our spirit for ever nomad, and would remain at war with the husbandman in us until all the hunter personified was given its rightful place again in our reckoning. The balance between those two had never been fairly and honourably struck, and until it was, we would remain as disastrously at war with ourselves as we had been with the Bushmen in the world without.

Indeed, I think one of the main causes of the uncompromising ferocity with which the Bushman had been persecuted originated precisely in the fact that he was a living image of what we had rejected and betrayed of our own aboriginal spirit. We had hoped unconsciously perhaps that if we killed him off in the world we would no longer be reminded of our deed of betrayal and could be at peace with ourselves. But of course we reckoned without our host in the form of this other Bushman charge in our inborn spirit. Where our history had so singularly failed was in not seeing that the reckoning could have as great a positive as a negative result. The negative we knew only too well from the story of the Bushman, and needed no emphasis; the positive did and was manifest in the effect of Hans Taaibosch on a person like herself and her countrymen. Hans Taaibosch proved that his race, given half a chance, could provoke as great a compassion as enmity.

She had demonstrated it already so movingly, I begged her to accept. Even in that unique child-man shape she and I loved so well he was an image and evocation of the state of being recommended to us in the New Testament, the exhortation to become like children again if we were ever to find the way to the united kingdom life called Heaven. Imperfect as the thought was and even more imperfectly expressed, I hoped that this interpretation of her devotion to Hans Taaibosch and her concern for an exile of a race so alien in their American midst would comfort her as it comforted, uplifted and stirred me.

And this time I put my hand on hers, held it firmly there until after a struggle with herself she thanked me almost inaudibly, sank into a silence again so deep that I had to lift her out of it. For the moment had come when I had to ask her the question that remained overwhelmingly unanswered between us. I was surprised how difficult it was even then because I was assailed by an uprising of emotion for which I was not prepared. I had only just seen Hans Taaibosch raised up into life between us and if the answer was what I feared would have to endure his end more swiftly without the immunity of someone who had already fore-suffered it all as she had. It was a transition so quick and extreme that my imagination shrank from it, yet I did manage to say, 'Please could you not *now* tell me what exactly became of him?'

DANCE OF THE GREAT HUNGER

Dance of the Great Hunger

'OF course, I must and will,' she began, her voice for the first time harsh and almost matter-of-fact, because of stricture of her own recollected sadness of what had to come, and knowing exactly how it could get in the way of words again. 'But in order to do so properly you must please tell me what dancing would have meant to Hans Taaibosch, because it was very important at the end and I'd like to know the answer if possible before I go on. You did say at Pendle Hill that they were great dancers, didn't you?'

'It meant almost as much as their stories and even painting,' I told her quickly, anxious to take advantage of the opportunity the change of tone her voice suggested we now had of overcoming our inner hesitations and returning to the reality of the present, however brutal it might be. Indeed I found an unexpected ally in that I had not realized until then how I had longed to escape from this brooding, sullen atmosphere not only of Bushman history but of what we suspected Hans Taaibosch's life had been before he appeared so strangely in this skyscraper world, and to re-emerge in some fresh and new conclusion. It was almost as if all the atmospheric detail of human imperfection and tragedy implicit in Hans Taaibosch's life and the history of his people extracted in those long conversations between us since we had first

109

met and talked in the lamp-lit doorway on the edge of the night at Pendle Hill were gathered together around us there like the clouds of a great storm, depressive and heavy upon us and in need now of some lightning thrust of fact to shake them with thunder and make the rain fall at last, as the Bushmen themselves would have had it in one of their greatest images of meaning.

'Yes, they loved dancing so much that they had a dance for everything. Where their words, stories and paintings failed them, their dancing took over. It was almost as if they knew how the great unknown and imponderables of their lives had to be acted out, to be lived fully to the end in a way for which the dancing was sponsor, before it could be known and another great fragment of universal mystery transformed into living wonder. So they danced as perhaps only the stars and Shiva danced at the heart of the stillness of the darkness to shake it into light. Of course it was not the dancing you see at the Bolshoi, Covent Garden or the City Ballet of New York, but for me, who's seen dancing at all those places, it was far more moving. He would dance, for instance, the story of man's search for fire and his sense of liberation, gratitude and reverence when with the help of mantis he found his fire at last. He would dance his joy at the birth of a child and his anguish at the death of a friend. He would dance out his gratitude to the animal his hunter had brought home for having been so good to allow itself to be killed so that he could continue to live. There was nothing he did not have a dance for. It was amazing that as he danced, usually only in the darkest hour of the night, the fact that he was dancing conveyed itself to all nature around him, not only compelling it to recognize the rhythm but also to become a party to it.

'I remember, for instance, a night when they danced

their great fire dance and how, as the dance approached its climax towards midnight, the lions began to roar as I've never heard them before, almost as if keeping time with the stamping, dancing feet which made the desert reverberate like a drum, and harmonizing like great bass accompanists, with the voices of the women singing to keep their men dancing, and the sound rising clear, bright and lofty as the highest of the stars. In the end all of desert nature was drawn in, ostriches with their booming, night plovers with their deep-sea piping, owls with their solemn hooting and the night-jar with its castinet voices. And in the gaps between the waves of the swelling tide of sound, the night cicada sopranos could be heard like rows of seraphim and cherubim piled on top of one another, their song soaring until it seemed to me it reached high enough to stir the stars themselves and make them succumb to the rhythm below and go tap dancing all over the shining black floor of that desert heaven. In the end the dancing produced such an atmosphere of oneness and belonging between all that when the climax came and the fire was found I felt that I, who had come so far from so remote a world, was no longer a stranger, standing alone and isolated, but someone who had found sanctuary in an ancient temple participating for the first time in an act of natural Communion with one of the greatest congregations of life ever gathered.

'And then of course they danced in the same way to the full moon. When I asked them why, they would say, "You see that the moon which is sitting there so nicely, feeling itself to be so full of light is about to wither and fade and die utterly away and will not renew itself in dying and return again to us with such a heart full of light unless we here, feeling ourselves to be dancing thus, make her feel utterly how much our hearts belong to her and need her light to know our way in the darkness of life on earth." I mention this dance to the moon particularly because it shows perhaps most clearly of all what their dancing meant to them. For surely, what greater demonstration can you have of the importance attached to the art than an absolute conviction such as theirs, that the waxing and waning of even the moon is dependent on it? I could go on and on giving you examples like these — but I hope these will be enough to answer your question.'

She made it clear at once that she had understood, for she exclaimed, 'Oh, how beautiful! Thank you, oh thank you for telling me that. I wouldn't have missed it for anything, but I hope you won't think me ungrateful or greedy,' she spoke so as to make light of things, in the way her kind does, of burdens its spirit finds hard to bear, 'but I have a particular dance in mind you haven't mentioned yet, or rather two similar ways of dancing that Hans had. It may not have been the greatest of your Bushman dances but to us, particularly as children, it made us very happy to watch him doing it. We were always asking him to repeat dances for us. And do you know, that dear, patient, generous little man never once said no. It was a peculiar sort of dance. He would take off his coat, undo his tie, remove his shirt, take off his shoes and socks and stand there in his bare feet, with only his trousers firmly belted round his peculiar little middle. He would put out his hands wide in front of him, give a kind of lion-like growl, and begin stamping his feet. Then, in the centre of his stomach, we would see all his muscles coming together in a sort of ball and jerk to the left side of his body. And this ball of muscle would then suddenly begin to dance from one side to the other, up and down and down and up, continuously and vigorously as if it were an entity of its own, matching the rhythm of those flashing, dancing, stamping little feet. I can't tell you what excitement this dance produced in us. Have you any idea from your own experience what sort of a dance I mean?'

I did not answer directly because there was something I had to know before I could give her the answer as with a feeling of excitement I believed I could. So I said, 'You spoke as if there might have been two, not just one dance. What was the difference in the dancing that made you say this? I would be very grateful if you could tell me every detail because it is extremely important.'

'It was just this,' she answered quickly, 'that sometimes he danced in this way I described, with his neck forward, head bowed and eyes searching around the ground at his feet, and his hands moving rhythmically towards the floor in grasping little gestures, but in the other his head was thrown well back and his eyes raised upwards with an expression I would say of a longing that made me want to cry, and his hands stretched as high as they could, palms wide open, fingertips trembling as if he were pleading, begging, praying to something high up beyond his and our vision. The strange thing was that the first kind of dancing I've described to you was the kind he did most often when I first met him as a child, but as he grew older he did less and less of it, and in the end whenever we asked him to dance, he only danced the one with his hands stretched to their utmost length up to the sky. I assure you that this had nothing to do with ailing physical power and decline of vigour because this last variation was every bit if not more exacting than the first. Does that help?'

This last question was once more dark with a return of an anxiety as of a mother for the fate of a lost child,

113

A Mantis Carol

which seemed endemic in the attitude of this woman towards Hans Taaibosch, and I was glad that for once I could answer, certain of my authority.

'The first dance you describe is the dance of the little hunger,' I told her confidently. 'The second variation they call the dance of the great hunger. They are two of their greatest dances, and significantly danced as a rule not collectively but by one dancer alone as if to indicate that whatever the dance means, it is peculiarly a matter for him and his own fate and not for others to join in and interfere. They are the great terminal dances of Bushman life. The first one is of the physical hunger the child experiences the moment he is born and satisfies first at his mother's breast, and which from then on stays with him for the rest of his life on earth. But the second dance is the dance of a hunger that neither the food of the earth nor the way of life possible upon it can satisfy. It is a dance of the Bushman's instinctive intimation that man cannot live by bread alone, although without it he cannot live at all; hence the two.

'Whenever I asked them about this great hunger they would only say, "not only we dancing, feeling ourselves to be raising the dust which will one day come blown by the wind to erase our last spoor from the sand when we die, lest others coming and seeing our footsteps there might still think us alive, not only we feel this hunger, but the stars too, sitting up there with their hearts of plenty, they too feel it and feeling it, tremble as if afraid they would wane and their light die, on account of so great a hunger. Grand Mother Sirius, sitting there with the greatest heart of plenty, sitting higher than all the rest, feeling herself to be looking over the edge of the night into the day beyond, knows this hunger too and seeing how far and long we must travelling go together

114

before this hunger can be killed, weeps for us all who are dear to her heart, and lets her tears falling come to splash in the dust kicked up by our dancing feet and lie on the bushes and grass, so that we in the morning seeing how white and shining their leaves have become, know that they are wet and glistening thus with star-tears shed in the night because of this great hunger and us on account of it." '

Although I knew my rendering of a Bushman answer heard however often so many years before was by no means complete, I could vouch for the exactitude of the feelings they left in me and was reassured to see how much the answer meant to her. And yet I have never regretted more that there is no substitute for experience in life, because I longed for her to have experienced it all as I had done, so that she who had done so much to earn the right of the ultimate vision, could know how Hans Taaibosch in his preference for this dance of the great hunger to all others in his advancing years was being obedient to the pattern of departure and return which, deepest as I believe it to be of all the patterns of our spirit, goes perhaps deepest of all in those of us raised and fashioned out of the scarlet dust of Africa.

For consider; all she had told me made it clear that Hans Taaibosch's dancing in the beginning put all the stress on the hunger felt at the point of departure but ended by a shift of the emphasis to the dance of the hunger beyond the terminal of his final return, because no matter whether insect, bird, animal or human being in Africa, when the season of return is upon them and the round of flesh and blood on earth is nearing completion and the circle about to be tightly drawn, all living things long to go back also to the place where they were born. I have not only been told this by the people of Africa

speaking just for themselves. They say that it is true also
of all nature, speaking of it as they do in the vivid light
of their own experience and out of an act of almost mystical participation in the nature of the animal and all other
forms of being that encompass them. All, they say, as the
final hour approaches, long to complete the round by
joining their own thread of life to the place from which
it first began to circle.

Even I knew from my own pioneering family, stories
of old Bushman survivors who had fled for safety into the
wastelands of Africa, in their old age risking death in
penetrating stealthily the by now well-established settle-
ments of their enemies in order to return to some over-
hanging cliff or cave which had sheltered them as children.
There they were seen by enemies compassionate enough
not to betray them to their communities, so moved were
they by the sight of these old people pressing their wrinkled cheeks against the rocks, fondling the boulders,
stroking and touching all round them tenderly with the
tips of their fingers and weeping bitterly as if they were
long lost living things found after a heart-breaking search.

Hans Taaibosch must have known, of course, must
have accepted the fact 'utterly' as he would have said,
that for him there could be no physical return ever to his
place of birth to welcome him at the end. He could only
return to it in the spirit, and the most effective way was
to dance out his longing to look on the place of his origin
for the last time, and dance and re-dance this deep, deep
pattern of departure and return, as his people had always
danced out the inexpressible, unbearable and unattain-
able in their cruel little round of life on earth. But I felt
I had said almost more than could be absorbed in so taut
a moment. In any case, judging by the expression on her
face, enough to help, so that I thought I could ask now

more lightly than before, 'But it is your turn now. Please tell me why you asked me about this kind of dancing, and what role did it finally play in your and Hans Taaibosch's life?'

'It was only this,' she said with the greatest of difficulty, using the 'only' not reductively but as a substitute for a sense of it having been all of everything that could possibly ever have mattered at the time. 'It was only — ' and she hesitated again before adding in that maddeningly indirect way of hers. 'Did I ever tell you that he called all the girls and women he knew Dolly?'

'No,' I answered, I fear with some impatience, because I had had enough atmosphere and needed some simple, uncomplicated facts. 'No, you've not mentioned it before.'

'Oh, how remiss of me,' she exclaimed, genuinely contrite. 'You see, he called us all, even me, Dolly, though he knew very well what my name was. The last time I visited him he was very ill in bed and I sat with him and held his hand while he was lying there breathing heavily, his old face looking more wrinkled than ever and his eyes firmly shut. I don't know how long I sat there except that I went on doing so gladly because I knew he knew I was there, so firmly was he holding my hand. Suddenly he opened his eyes and he smiled at me not as an old man but as he smiled when I first met him in the prime of his life. He said in a voice almost young with the note of gaiety in it, "Dolly, dance for me, please. Please dance for me Dolly, I have so often danced for you." And the strange thing was that all my instincts were to get up and dance for him the dance of the great hunger, as you've called it, in the manner he had so often done for us, only I didn't know half the how of it, never having danced it myself. But his eyes were so full of expectation and so pleading that I thought; Oh heck, come what may

117

and no matter what a fool I make of myself, I'll do my best for him.

'I let his hand go, stood up, saw his eyes following me eagerly, kicked off my shoes, stepped into the centre of the room and turned my back on him, as he had always done, to begin with a great sideways stamping on the floor with his bare feet before he would whirl about to confront us with his face and hands thrown upwards. But in turning my back on him, I heard a strange sound, like the issue of some gust of great wind thrown at the door with such force that it passed thin and elongated through the key-hole into and out of the room. It was a sound I'd never heard before, but it filled me with alarm. I instantly whirled about, and Hans Taaibosch had gone.

'I say gone, not as an evasion of fact but deliberately because I felt then, although I can only put it into words tonight because of what you have told me, that his spirit in that moment had recovered the freedom of movement so vital to it and gone on a great long walk-about of the universe which he had rehearsed so well and loved so much on earth, and that he was not, as the doctor who was immediately summoned declared him to be, dead . . . '

WALK-ABOUT

Walk-about

EXPECTED as the end was, the manner of Hans Taaibosch's going and this woman's tender share in it
moved me so much that I felt totally unmanned. I could
only bow my head and hold it in my hands in silence
before the weight of the dignity and generosity of spirit
of it all. I knew that I ought to say something, however
banal, as acknowledgement of the importance of what I
had heard and not wait until I felt capable of expressing
all the complexities and nuances made suddenly so single
and clear in the focus of such an end, but I could not
trust myself even to the best of the platitudes prescribed
for such occasions.

She had to break the silence and ask, obviously perturbed by my reaction, 'I do hope you don't think I was
splitting hairs or trying to evade the reality of what had
happened by a mere euphemism, when I said that Hans
had merely gone from me and was not "dead". The distinction mattered enormously to me then. It came to me
unbidden and goes on to matter as much as ever. I would
hate you to think it was anything less.'

I looked up at her then. I must have expected to see
a face as wet with tears as it must have been on the day
Hans Taaibosch left her world, but her eyes were wider,
clearer and brighter than ever, making me realize how
there are feelings neither words nor tears can express

121

A Mantis Carol

because they issue sheer from the living fire of being where tears themselves are burnt away, no matter how fast and abundantly they are formed. Her example somehow rearmed me. I do not remember the exact words I used then because despite the long, random years in between, the emotion which accompanied them was so powerful that I cannot yet recall it with sufficient tranquillity to recollect totally and with clarity what happened. But I do believe I could have left no doubt in her mind that the distinction for me too was valid. Hans Taaibosch for me too was only technically dead, had merely gone on somewhere beyond space and time which for all the authority and immensity of their concepts are merely provisional outposts of human awareness on its far frontier with an undiscovered world of infinite possibilities of new being and meaning. Yes, somewhere out there in an inconceivable dimension with no inhibitions of time or space, I was convinced that Hans Taaibosch or, more precisely, the imperishable image made visible through him that once fashioned his unique child-man shape and fired it with clear, unembittered spirit, was once more, as he would have put it, on the spoor of whatever it was in the teeming unknown that could minister to this great hunger so often made demonstrable in his dancing, and shared, in so full a measure of his devout imagination, with the stars and all the other systems wheeling in their several courses towards a single end. If that were not so, I begged her to believe, he could not have lived for me as he had done in that room.

It was as if he had been born of her in that room. She had conceived of all that was true, timeless and imperishable in Hans Taaibosch, so that he could be reborn, nursed and mothered with the tender care of the most fastidious and precious of feminine intuitions until I felt

122

Walk-about

I had met him in the flesh, seen him alive and grow old and accompanied him to stand with her at the exit of his world. I could not thank her enough for that, although I would not, indeed could not yet try to define how and why immediately.

I do not know what kind of reaction she had finally expected from me but I suspect it was less than this. From the way she looked and thanked me through a blur of tears I was certain she had feared disappointment to a degree I was incapable of fathoming, so that today it is as if it were only yesterday that I heard her saying again, almost praying to herself, her hands over her face, 'Dear God, what a relief, what a blessed relief. Hans, we have company at last.'

And when, after a while, she took her hands away and looked up at me clear-eyed again, she explained how for years she had lived with this strange feeling of Hans Taaibosch being still alive after a fashion and insisting that there was something she must still do for him; something only she could do. She thought the feeling would pass in time because there seemed no rational sense in it and perhaps only one of the forms her grief at his going would naturally take.

Yet she tried with all the sensitivity and imagination she could summon to discern what she might perhaps have left undone in Hans's life and of which his memory could be demanding some sort of recognition from her. But she could not think of a single thing, except of course the many little failures of deed and omission of which the best of us are guilty in our relationships with one another. Still, the feeling did not only increase but kept her awake at night, so much so that she was convinced some essential part of the point of her own life would be lost unless she could find out what it could mean.

123

She had almost given up hope until she came to the talks at Pendle Hill. She had never heard of me and came purely because she had read in her newspaper that I too was of Africa as Hans Taaibosch had been. A Quaker herself, she had no difficulty in getting an invitation to take part in the talks. From the first talk she knew, and at the same time because of fear of disappointment felt she could not know for certain, that she was there to bring Hans and me together. The pull between the knowing and not knowing at times, she interjected, was almost unbearable. It was because of this feeling of such a mission that she had begged to talk to me, since it was as if she had been hearing Hans Taaibosch's funny little Bushman-English voice itself commanding her, so important was it to him, to be introduced to me.

'And I was right, more right than I could ever have hoped or imagined,' she exclaimed, clasping her hands in front of her. 'You cannot believe how suddenly deeply and utterly at peace I feel after all these years. I feel almost . . . ' She hesitated, as if the thought was so great, almost sacred, that any attempt at utterance might both diminish and profane it, before she took heart and went on, 'I feel almost that something of the great hunger has gone from him now that I've told you and you understand, because your understanding would add to the substance of his life. I think what I feared most was that he would vanish without trace, as it were, when I too died, and nothing or no one left to mark or remember how singular and remarkable he had been under the visiting moon he must have loved so well, judging by what you have told me.

'I feel now that you know and can give him a place in the record of his people, his life will not have been pointless but could pass on his little quota of meaning, though

124

what that meaning exactly is I could no more put in words than jump over the moon. Yet I'm positive it is there for the asking, because I have never felt such a blissful peace after years of tension within. I do hope you won't find all this exaggerated. It was the most extraordinary thing altogether by any standards, don't you think — the way he came and lived and ended up so happily in our midst? Yet every word I have told you about him is true.'

I reassured her that nothing, nothing seemed exaggerated to me in what she had said. Indeed her story was more extraordinary even than she could have imagined, so much so that it made the hair on the back of my head stand on end and left me with no pretence of being able to explain it to my own, let alone the satisfaction of our sort of world. All I could do was to add the strange, imponderable facts I knew to her account of his life and let them speak for themselves.

First there was one great fact of the history of human imagination to be taken into consideration of all this. Everywhere at all times, in all cultures and races of which we have record, when the greatest meaning, the highest value of life men called their gods or god, needed renewal and increase through life on earth, it began the process through a dream. For instance, the Iliad, one of the greatest of our own complex of stories that began the authentic adventure of the European spirit, starts on its fateful course with Zeus, the Greek god of gods in parliament on Olympus, inflicting a dream with purpose aforethought on the great fore-doomed Agammemnon, as he slept by his black ships on the yellow sand between the impounded white-horse beach and the rim of the great plain of Troy.

Then in the Old Testament too, that other great tributary of our own special Hebraic-Greek-Roman story, it was the dream of a God and a ladder of angels in the desert that was sent to comfort Jacob after his betrayal of Esau, to convey a promise of divine support for him on his side of this great divide in the human spirit, so relevant to all our bloody warring yesterdays and the story of Hans Taaibosch and the Bushman. The examples were without end of diversity or number, but always and everywhere the pattern was the same: in the beginning a dream. All that, I was afraid, might sound to her such archaic stuff, such old hat as to appear utterly irrelevant to the contemporary scene in which the Hans Taaibosch with whom she and I were so concerned, had appeared like a projection of prehistory. But it was not. I had told no one yet, except the dreamer concerned, that I would never have come to America had it not been because of a dream. Had it not been for a dream I would not be there now in a position to have received Hans Taaibosch's story from her.

Her eyes widened with astonishment. She sat up straight for the first time, outwardly as alert as hitherto she had been only inwardly. She would undoubtedly have spoken, had I not hastened to add that stranger still, it was a dream which although dreamt in America, had as principle the praying mantis, the god of the Bushmen and therefore of Hans Taaibosch. Indeed the praying mantis had not only figured in person in the dream at the beginning but continued to appear in dream after dream, year after year, to the same reluctant dreamer, just as Hans Taaibosch had pursued her year after year in her own mind and heart, refusing to take no for an answer and demanding that she should take note of him until in despair she wrote to me for help. It was a fact therefore, summing it up crudely, that if it had not been for mantis himself and his persistent, indefatigable dream visita-

tions, she would never have got herself, me and Hans
Taaibosch to meet. Now what in earth or Heaven did she
make of that?

She shook her head slowly and gravely and only said
in a voice low with weight of awe, 'Strange, how much
stranger than I could ever have thought . . . ' and re-
sumed her silence to stare at me expectant, her eyes
asking for more.

Would it be too fanciful to suppose, I went on therefore,
that mantis, or the greatest universal of which he was
one of the earliest and most enigmatic images, had initiated and manipulated us all — men, women, time, chance
and circumstance, despite all their built-in inertia to unlikely promptings and resistances to the unfamiliar, let
alone their and our own complexities and diversities —
to a single preconceived end? Only the exercise of some
such authority could account perhaps for the certainty
and minute sense of detail and clarity of direction which
made it impossible for us all not to meet for this purpose
as surely as we had. As for the role of Hans Taaibosch
in all this, it seemed as if he had been chosen as an
instrument for revealing to us an aspect of meaning that
was uniquely in the keeping of the master image mantis
himself represented and so through us to the life of our
time.

What else, for instance, could I make of the fact that
I, whom I believed without egotism or arrogance to be
the only person alive with the kind of experience necessary to understand something of what mantis stood for
in Bushman imagination and to know what Hans Taaibosch's unconfessed spirit had been about before he came
to America, seemed to have been deliberately brought
out to New York against my desire and conscious inten-
tions? And was it not more than just superstition to be

alive to the possibility that the imperishable image of Hans Taaibosch released from his provisional arrest in America which had haunted her so, could have been responsible for it all in the first instance? Could he not in his hunter's ardour on the spoor of nourishment for the great hunger, have solicited his god and connived with him to just such a purpose, as he did not hesitate to call on mantis for help when on the track of the game he needed for food on earth?

I had obviously put something in words which she had already intuitively intercepted in terms of her own feelings for she remarked, 'I can hardly dare to believe it yet but it feels not only possible — but deeply and firmly true. What other explanation could there be? Surely I couldn't feel it to be so absolutely true because I've so longed to be relieved from the apparent senselessness and incongruity of Hans's life with us? It can't be just wishful thinking or, more precisely, I don't honestly think I could be so ready to accept what you say just because it gives me some selfish satisfaction in appearing to confirm how right I was all along in my conviction that there was more in all this than met the eye. I was going to say more than one could have dreamt of — but that would be wrong now, seeing how all along dreaming was a vital part of it all. No, I accept completely that, as you said earlier on, we are in the presence of a great, living mystery. But what could the meaning of it be? Couldn't we find some words to give us some idea of it? Please try, because if you can't, no one ever can.'

I would try, I promised her as well as myself, and immediately made my first attempt.

THE CAROL

The Carol

FORTUNATELY, I had some inkling of what it could
mean. Although I already implied part of it in the
question I had put to her, I was certain now that this
pattern of coming and going, weaving and interweaving
of lives and cultures already apparent in the substance
of this conversation between us was neither casual nor
accidental. One or two coincidences, apart from my own
belief or prejudices in the matter as set out in the beginning, could have been regarded as not enough to satisfy
an upright and honourable spirit of pure reason, but there
were so many of them, great and small, woven into every
stage and aspect of the story, that any explanation of
their role in it as either casual or accidental had to be
rejected out of hand.

I was sustained in this by the fact that there was even
more to it than I had hinted at, so much more that we
might never know the 'how' and 'why' of it and would
have to stop worrying over the method of delivery and
content ourselves with a search for the message. But first,
I believed, we had to accept the mystery in full, take upon
ourselves the mystery of things in the way Shakespeare
would have put it, as if we were God's spies or, perhaps
more precisely in this instance, spies of mantis, and as
spies from behind the lines of unawareness, beyond the
boldest of those outposts of mind on the far frontiers of

the unknown where the image of Hans Taaibosch was
out tracking at this moment, we might bring some worthwhile intelligence back with us.

'But surely the mystery could not be greater than it
already is?' she exclaimed, protesting as if she would find
more excessive.

I told her that I was afraid it was. I struck a note of
warning because we had not dealt adequately with the
element of the timing of it all. That for me was perhaps
the strangest and subtlest and most difficult to define.
And to make it less intractable I had to tell her the detail
of the timing and coincidence which I have mentioned
in the course of the story, from the great seasonal syn-
chronicities to such niceties of parallel and counterpoint
as those evoked in sheer names, like those of the woman
whom mantis chose as his dreaming instrument and that
of my own arrested work on the heart of the hunter of
whom also mantis was the praying, watching, contem-
plative god.

She had listened all along with loyal respect but what
degree of conviction she would be able to bring to what
had now to come, I could not tell, since it was an aspect
I had not yet discussed with anyone and barely given
enough consideration to myself. I feared perhaps unjustly
that what I now wanted to say would raise the stature of
the mystery to a measure verging on the unacceptable
even to one as well disposed as herself. She appeared
astonished when I insisted that there was still more to
come. Indeed, I had just begun to point out how the most
significant piece of timing was with us there and now.
All seasons, time past and present and both our general
and particular histories seemed to me coincident and at
one in that room. I thought then that she was going to
interrupt and ask for clarification. As a result I found

myself provoked to interject rather abruptly, 'But you do realize what the hour is, don't you?'

She obviously misunderstood me for she raised her hand so fast to look at the watch on her own wrist that the light glanced off the metal like an arrow of gold.

'I know it is always later than we think,' she answered instantly apologetic. 'But I never thought it could be as late as this. It is just past one. And I think I must go. It's much too late to go on, perhaps some other time . . . '

She looked hurt, disappointed, ruffled, frustrated, contrite and dismayed as if she felt she had failed in her purpose, and all in one, complex glance. I hastened to reassure and make amends to her. It was never too late in this level of life we were discussing. It was not the time recorded on watches I was concerned with; it was the season and character of time itself. Did she realize it was the first hour in the morning of 22nd December? The old Chinese had a proverb that at midnight noon was born. One hour ago the noon of a new season, of a new spring in the world, had been born in the night outside. The day before was the shortest of the year, when our ration of light was the smallest, and night the longest, and the darkness the greatest. Yet at such a moment of extremity in time when to all appearances there seemed to be no reason why the darkness should not go on increasing and the light diminishing until it vanished altogether, the whole movement of time was reversed and the universe bound for a whole hour already on a new course towards a decline of the dark and an increase of light. Did she realize that spring was already one hour old?

So much for the moment and its place in the character of time but what of its position in history and its synchronicity in the life of man, particularly of Hans Taaibosch and ourselves? Historically it was many things but for us in particular it was the beginning of Christmastide. Could she perhaps not see now why just such a moment of extremity was chosen and could be the only possible timing appropriate for the event of Christmas? Some two thousand years ago in the darkest night of the human soul, a tide of life had turned at just such an hour and the noon of new season in the spirit of man born, as spring was being born, in the universal night around it. Up to that precise minute and second, the life of man could not have been more at the mercy of a slanted half of itself masquerading as a whole on the other side of the great divide of which we had spoken. Man was utterly at the mercy of a way of life based on wordly power, altogether arrested, worn out and incapable of renewal and increase, however great its contribution to the life of man at its best had been before.

Then suddenly, out of a despised, rejected and persecuted area of a natural self of man on the far side of the great divide out in the dark of life, among bitter clouds of unknowing, the noon of a new way of life, a new source of power was born. Yes, it had a name, I added quickly, to arrest the sound I saw forming on her lips, but let us leave the name aside until we had done with the time and the imagery instrumental to it and come to the place where it belonged and first found its most authoritative expression. Consider that there could have been no better personification of the birth of a despised and rejected self than in that of a child born, in terms of the world of power, illegitimately to a woman of the most despised, persecuted and rejected race of the day, the Jews. And this imagery of rejection was reinforced, re-emphasized and put beyond question by the fact that the child personifying the rejection lived to be doubly rejected, indeed eliminated by the rejected people themselves and the very element in life he had come to rescue from their arrested selves.

Could anything have demonstrated better the absence of what he was to represent in the life of his time than the fact that there was no room for his labouring mother even in the meanest wayside hospice or inn? Could one imagine a better illustration of his emergence from what is truly in the nature of natural man uncorrupted by power and possessions and property than his birth among animals in the stable? One had to be careful not to raise the parallel to an absurd and too exalted a plane, but could she not see how Hans Taaibosch too, as a despised and rejected natural person born of a persecuted race, was charged in his own small way with similar imagery? And was it not most significant therefore that all had been synchronized, so that Hans Taaibosch could be resurrected and she and I be searching for the meaning of his life there in America among them, just as we were nearing to the celebration of the day on which some two thousand years ago this new principle of life so vulnerable and defenceless in that great Roman day, was made flesh and blood at just such a moment too, when the universe was once more compelling a new season in the character of time out there in the greatest darkness of the year shut out by that curtained window behind her? We too were living in another Roman hour of time with life under arrest crying for a renewal and rebirth in every aspect of itself. So what could such a coincidence of timing then and now here suggest, I asked, except a clear intimation that in this birth of a new principle, the movement in the heart of man in time, and the turning over of the seasons, were at one, joined to a common end?

Could one doubt any longer, after such a coincidence

and coming together of time, man, history, the universe and all its systems and seasons, that they were not all subject to the rule of one, overriding and common law?

It was as much as she could take because, she broke in a voice firm and commanding, 'And this new principle, what is it? Hans was not religious in the conventional sense and he was certainly not a Christian. So how can it apply to him and what can you mean?'

His absence of a conventional or Christian approach to religion was unimportant, I told her. The important thing was that he was a naturally religious person. Had he not danced out his sense of religion for her time and time again in his dance of the great hunger?

She supposed readily that he had, but what was that great hunger specifically about?

It was my turn now to be anxious, because, although I knew it with a certainty and clarity I have seldom experienced about anything, I was reluctant to name it. I was afraid, because almost since the moment of the coming of the word in the beginning, the name has been used so much and so badly, even as a label for states of mind and spirit that contradicted what it was formed to express, that it had become one of the most misunderstood words in the history of man. In our day, particularly, like all words that become part of popular currency where their own integrity of meaning is daily assailed by overuse and imprecise and over-generalized application, it might in the process of inflation which the process produces, have lost value to such an extent as to pass out of the realm of meaning, were it not for the fact that there is no substitute for it in speech as there is no alternative for it in life. Afraid as I was of the reductive consequences its use would have, not in the spirit of this woman, but in the minds of others whom I hoped would consider what I put on record of our encounter, I had no option but to prepare to tell her that the name of this great hunger was the hunger for love and for a way of life lived in love out of love for the love of it alone.

Yet before I could utter it, I experienced a violent and explosive rebellion of spirit against the level of time she had not long ago taken note of on her watch, that most shallow and frivolous one-dimensional aspect of one of the most profound of our realities, because I knew I had no time in that unilateral sense to describe some of the special nuances that the word held for me, for all my longing to do so. I had no time for instance to remind her of the wonderful affirmations of it in Paul's letter to the young Corinthian church, where he so movingly and truly declared this great mystery which had just been demonstrated in a crucifixion, to be the highest of all values, before going on to the tentative ones, revealed in the search for its meaning in my own errant and inadequate life.

In a way, Hans Taaibosch had summed up much of it for me better than I could do in words, by dancing it as a hunger which the whole universe and all that there is of life within it experiences all the time. But had he danced out the paradox of it; how it was both great hunger and food of its own hunger at one and the same time? I believed not. So how could she know, as I believed I knew, how no life can be brought out from the cold and dark on the other side of this great divide which had split man against himself, into the light and warmth of our day so that the unlived could be lived, the unreal made real and some greater new being conceived so that when delivered to us and lived in accordance with it, life would be more bright, clear, precise, immediate and at one with itself, time, and the wheeling universe, than before?

137

A Mantis Carol

Could she know that it was the only great reconciling factor that could bring together those two opposites of man so long and so disastrously at war with one another since this division in the beginning, and that, once joined, they would form a unity not of two but of three which to our reason would appear as untrue as it was impossible, because of its demonstrable mathematical absurdity?

That was part of the mystery because, in the mathematics of this love, addition was achieved by subtraction and two or even three needed to make a one. That is why perhaps a poet not understanding the paradoxical arithmetic of love, had once declared that because two and two had always made four and never five, the heart of man had long been sore. He did not know this mathematics of meaning which made mere addition subtraction, and the surrender and sacrifice which was a subtraction of ourselves, a multiplication of many into one. I myself did not know about two and two but I did know how one and one could make three to become a one again in the dimension of love, and the heart of man less sore on account of it.

And then could she know as I knew that the falsest of the many false things said about it was the statement that it was blind? Of course one knew how well intentioned a statement it was but none the less love overlooked nothing. For me that was crucial, because I believed it to be wide-eyed and open, with a vision full and unafraid, surveying the whole immense field of life from before the beginning to beyond the end, using again two highly provisional and suspect terms of limitation that are only too human and mortal, since there are no others to serve our own allotment of meaning. For me it could not be less blind. It was the clearest of visions unclouded by the unknowing of the moment and unblurred by experience of failure in the past, remaining focused with the certainty and lucidity of knowledge complete and precise of what was to come and had to be. We knew life and it only in part, but it knew both of us and what we could and had to become in full. It was nothing if not a commitment without reservation to our and the universe's greater becoming.

Indeed, so clear was its vision, and certain its knowledge of the whole, that it could look in to each and every part that was the object of its love, no matter how great or infinitessimal, discern all their several inadequacies, imperfections and even the denial of itself in any given phase of evolution of the misguided entity and yet emerge at the end of its scrutiny neither disillusioned, deceived, disappointed nor repulsed but with its love for all that had failed it not just intact but increased according to the measure of their lack and need of it.

It was all this because it was history, time and space transcended in terms of its one, great and for ever now. Time, if only we could feel it again, as it sang within our blood, was not just a lineal measure but the beat of the heart of love, the rhythm of its growth and increase in life, the rate of its advance and its patience in the conversion of error and redemption of imperfection, so that when all error has been corrected, all imperfection redeemed and life made precise with love, there will be no need of time, and time will pass away and another dimension will come to take its place. But love will stay.

Even the sky, stretched to where the last faint spawn of a new Andromeda starring mist smoked a million light years away to blur the black on the horizon of the most powerful lens peering into our great surround of darkness, was only roof of a wayside tent, shutting out a greater mystery of love beyond. Space itself, in which the

tent is pitched, was only one of the sites of many camps
on its march to fulfillment. The day itself was sheer love
of darkness for light conceived in a dream of delivery
from the prison of itself in the sleep of the night, so that
it was no longer sterile and alone but the rest to which
the day after one fulfilment of it could return to be re-
freshed in a new dream of greater illumination of the
black. It was the improbable spring in the intractable
heart of winter.

And yet how say all this and so much more when
millions today were conditioned to it largely as an indulgence of physical senses, although it could never be
overlooked that even so minor an exercise of its reality
too was evidence of its vigilance and power and that no
one could escape its service altogether, even if only in
service after so inadequate a fashion, so that afterwards
all were uneasy with suspicion that it was much more
than a kiss against some technicolour sunset. Against so
lush, plush a background of contemporary evaluations,
how convey that it was infinitely heroic and its calling to
its subjects utterly objective and that it was as tough as
it was tender, as demanding as it was giving, as supple
as it was of the temper of steel forged for battle, and so
much else at one and the same paradoxical instant?

Whoever heeded its calling was daily in battle from the
moment he stepped out of bed, not for what was or is,
however good, but for what had to come. Neither happiness nor unhappiness were more than by-products of
its movement through life. It was something greater than
either and that was a meaning which, if loved as it loves
life, served as it serves, has at its disposal the greatest
transforming energies of which man, life and his universe are capable. So great that even the agony and apparent end in the crucifixion of the one life lived exclusively

in its service, was transcended by a joy of mission accomplished which still passed human understanding and left those who took note of it humble and reverent in the presence of a mystery, which although they can never know it or experience it in full, still through its nearness invest their own partial lives with known and living wonder.

Alas, I felt to my everlasting reproach and shame that I had no time to put any of this to her and consider her response to it. I could only seek reassurance in the fact that this mystery of love is for me, as it was for Dante, a feminine mystery, and so would have its importance admitted by her instantly out of her own nature as woman without aid of the conceptualization men find so necessary for their access to meaning.

So I remarked, gently, feeling incredibly lame and inept, 'The great hunger, of course, is the hunger for love, and I am certain now that the point of Hans Taaibosch's apparently so irrelevant appearance in your world was to bear witness in his obscure way to the reality and power of love.'

I do not know what she had expected. All I know is that I had not put my trust in vain in that essence of woman in her, and should not have been surprised, seeing how it already had proved itself. I should not have needed any reminder of how inexperienced, alone and unarmed and with no warning to prepare this element in herself, she had been challenged by Hans Taaibosch in a metaphor and allegory of physical shape and spirit so unfamiliar and odd that they might have made his exclusion from such a vision automatic. Yet she had none the less seen immediately through the disguise and illusion of appearance to look straight into the heart of a cruelly abandoned and uncared for orphan of life, and compelled

A Mantis Carol

that sole consideration to over-ride all the values and
conventions of her established world, to reach out to it
instinctively with just such a love and take him into its
keeping.

As a result, all that within her responded immediately
and without reservation to what I had just said. I saw
understanding revealed on her face and in her eyes with
such speed that she seemed like someone who, wander-
ing in the dark of a great storm, suddenly in one flash of
searing lightning, had an immense landscape exposed
before her, instantly rediscovering her own lost footpath
woven like a thread of gold into the phosphorescent earth
at her feet. Indeed she sat looking at me speechless, not
seeing me, as if still not ready to go on, looking more
than ever poignantly young, vulnerable, exposed and unaware of the courage of love she had shown in her battle
for the unlikely being of Hans Taaibosch and still igno-
rant of the fact of how true an ambassador of the kingdom
of love she had been in the remote world of his spirit.

Had I been the relevant character in one of my favourite Dostoevsky stories, I think I would have got up,
knelt at her feet and when she, as she would no doubt
have done, had drawn back, protesting, I would have
answered, 'I do not bow down to you alone but to all the
love of life in time and space and expanding universe
that is represented in you and in what you felt and did
for Hans Taaibosch.'

Indeed I must have had some such heraldic impulse
since the impulse and the manner of it are prescribed in
an article beyond repeal in the ancient law of all living
things. Although it is in the nature of the masculine to
possess the will and the armour, it needs the feminine
to evoke the love of the whole that will give it the em-
ployment of meaning in life once called knightly, so that

142

on occasions such as this, when those elements of masculine and feminine meet, the imagination immediately experiences the transformation which was once called chivalrous. Not surprisingly, therefore, some acknowledgement in an antique gesture appeared called for just then. But I dismissed it as soon as it arose because I feared that to someone without my associations with such an act, it might seem over-theatrical.

Hard on that I had an even clearer impulse to get out of my chair and simply to thank her with an embrace. But the thought of how the greatest example of the kind of life I had in mind was betrayed by a kiss, made me dismiss it as readily as the first. Instead I took her right hand in mine and put it to my lips briefly, before saying, 'Yes, the great hunger he danced for you was the hunger of life for love, and I have no words, and can only thank you inadequately in this way as a sign of gratitude, on behalf of life, for how much you did for Hans Taaibosch in his almost intolerable share and denial of food of that hunger.'

Even this much, so little in comparison with what I felt her due, made her shy and so withdrawn that she could hardly get out the words, 'Of course I loved Hans but surely it was not all that important, certainly not enough for you to thank me as if it were something great or extraordinary. The lawyer, his family who gave him shelter and all those plain, ordinary circus people, they loved him as well. I was only one of many. You see . . . '

'Of course, I acknowledge their role and thank them too,' I tried to answer matter of fact, but soon dived back into the mainstream of the emotion evoked, 'I find it impossible to say in a few words what I feel, that so great a number of so-called ordinary people in your country could have been so extraordinary in their obedience to such an unlikely call on their love. I shall always remember them with gratitude and renewed hope of human life because of what they did for him. Yet they were for me the messengers of the love I have mentioned — you, its ambassador. I say this because only you thought it important enough to continue your investigation into the nature of his strange appearance, life, state of spirit and mind, after he had gone, and tried to evaluate the consequence of his death in a foreign land, carrying on the ambassadorial duties even to the minute detail of trying to discover his next of kin, of whom in a way I am one, so that you could report your news and findings to them, and ensure that the implications of his coming and going were assessed on his own indigenous level. Does that help to make my feelings clear?'

'Yes, in a way it does,' she replied touchingly. I say touchingly because already I thought that the more obedience to love seemed unremarkable to the obedient, the greater and more extraordinary in reality their portion of it in their heart. Indeed, how much she lacked a recognition of having done anything remarkable emerged clearly after the briefest of hesitations, as she added.

'But I still do not understand why you say you thank me on behalf of life. It's a mighty big thing to say for what I did.'

'No, it is nothing of the kind,' I told her firmly. 'This story of Hans Taaibosch, what led up to our meeting and your part in it all, is one of the most significant happenings of my own longish and not uneventful life. Although I know it is late and you are tired, I hope you'll bear with me if I tell you why, because all comes to a point in this.'

And thinking to myself, 'to hell with time and all watches who think they know what it's about,' I went on to try and explain with all the precision and fullness of which

144

The Carol

I was capable, what I had in mind. I began by meeting her question on the first of the three levels on which at the very least it had to be considered, if it were to be answered with any adequacy. I asked her to begin by considering the proposition with which the exterminators of the Bushmen and other races akin to them like the aborigines of Australia, their own Red Indians and countless others, justified the extermination. It was summed up in the phrase we both had objected to so much, 'they refused to be tamed'. Could she accept how it would seem as if the greatest of all meanings in life, of which mantis was the earliest of plenipotentiaries, had decided that life had suffered enough and far too long from so great a sham and decided to take up the challenge of the fraudulent proposition and expose it for the lie it was? Moreover it appeared to have done it deliberately in so extreme a form with the odds so much in favour of the sponsors of the lie and so much against its chosen challenger that no one would be able to doubt the outcome if the challenger won.

For consider the fact how the Hans Taaibosch who for me now appeared to have been chosen for just such an end, was first deprived of even the miserable prehistoric armoury he possessed before being confronted with the challenge. He was first torn out of context of his race, uprooted in spirit and being and, after a long apprenticeship in exile among alien societies, hostile in his interpretations within the deed and act of life, was constantly exposed, unaided and alone, to their shattering impact of denigration, starvation and erosion of his own natural spirit to be thrown ultimately into the swollen stream of life in the city of New York. And if she could tell me of any other place in the world which represented life based on an opposite of the one into which Hans Taaibosch had been born in a more extreme and overwhelming form than New York, I would like her to tell me of it.

She shook her head and murmured something to the effect that she had not thought of it like that before, but saw it all now and wrenched from herself the exclamation, 'Poor Hans! Poor, poor, dear little man!'

'Yes, poor Hans, but also lucky, fortunate, blessed Hans,' I added, 'because he came out of this trial, extreme as it was, a clear winner. Surely you must see this now and know why?'

She would only admit tentatively that she saw a glimmer of what it might portend without knowing why.

'He showed in a way no one could ever doubt again that there is no divide in the human spirit so deep that cannot be bridged if it submits itself to love,' I tried to make her accept. 'He made the grade, as you would say here, from the Stone Age to the contemporary day without loss of dignity or clarity of spirit because for the first time in his own life — no, of anyone in the life of his race — he experienced love. Love was all along all that he and his people needed to surmount any challenge that could be thrown at them in their prehistoric Stone-Age state.'

I thought her still not convinced that such love as they had given Hans Taaibosch so spontaneously could have been responsible for victory in the unequal context. So I elaborated on my belief, or rather the certainty of knowledge I felt, because it was based on my own experience and observation of life, to say that there was no challenge, however great, reckless or cataclysmic in its onslaught, that a spirit in full possession of love could not overcome.

And so this took the discussion on into the second level I thought essential. I said that Hans Taaibosch, in demolishing this long-established lie of history, exposed another great falsehood of our time which if left uncorrected would have results as disastrous to ourselves as it had so far been for so many other vanished civilizations. It was the current lie that man was a creature made solely by his environment. What he made of himself, the quality of his life, was held as a truth beyond dispute, dependent entirely on his environment and mechanism of his systems. One could only change man for the better, so ran the argument in the ascendent now, by changing his environment and systems. Could she not see how Hans Taaibosch's life exposed that too for the lie it was?

No one assessed in the scrutiny of those who propounded this spurious doctrine could have had so unfavourable an environment and so poor a start as Hans Taaibosch. I myself might have a tendency to regard life in the desert which was the last refuge of Hans Taaibosch's people as not a bad preparatory or even comprehensive school in terms of the wider plan of life, but, in the immediate tactical considerations of the progenitors of the lie, his beginning could not have been more unfavourable. So this challenge too had been taken up in his life in its most extreme form, and again he had emerged the victor. Provided there was love and an experience of love, the result implied, environment and systems were of relative unconcern; the worst of environments and most inept of systems could also further the good of man provided they were invested and used with love.

And then again there were those strange vendettas of history fought out in our time and a generation of life which had done nothing to beget or provoke them — the class, racial, cultural and other conflicts that made so great a shambles of the contemporary scene. They were excused and explained away because we were asked to consider them as a natural consequence of the injustice

147

one class, caste, race, or group of men had inflicted on another in the past. That too was shown up for the lie it was by Hans Taaibosch. Who could have had a longer past of such sustained and great injustice inflicted on them than he and his people? If the assumption were true, he should have been full to the brim and overflowing with a spirit of hatred and revenge. On the contrary, once exposed to the experience of love, there was no room for past or present hatred left in him, and space only for a growing disposition towards sweetness and yet more love. It was proof of how love was the only source of a spirit incapable of corruption either by wordly power or suffering. Could she not see how life had been a prisoner in a chain-gang of mere action and reaction to what was inflicted on it, because it was denied a power that was proof against these two great forces of corruption in history. If it were ever to be freed from a process that was a sort of perpetual Corsican feud against itself, it could only be through a surrender to a state of spirit immune to erosion either by suffering or corruption of power over others. Love, I knew, was such a force and Hans Taaibosch's life among them had instinctively made the truth of it manifest.

Hans Taaibosch's story, I stressed, implied as no specific life I had encountered yet, that civilized men used history partially and untruthfully to justify their fear and evasion of love. They sheltered behind it dishonourably like frightened, delinquent children behind the skirts of an ample mother, afraid to come out in the open and be themselves. As a result they became full of envy and malice to those who were out in life already on their own alone in the battle for love. That was the most sinister aspect for me about our time; its blindness to how our yesterdays had failed us not so much because of their inadequate bequest and their clumsy systems and short-comings but because of their denial of love.

This denial today had reached such proportions that increasing numbers of men, indeed whole societies and nations were not only incapable of experiencing love in themselves but of not even recognizing it when held out to them by others, seeing in the world around them nothing but evidence of the hatred and envy that impelled them from within. But it was a denial that could not be blamed on nature. It was estrangement from their own natural selves and what was left of the natural life around them that was the cause of it, for what could have been closer to natural man and aboriginal nature than Hans Taaibosch?

Consider how, without conscious effort or precept, he had been wide open to the experience of love and capable of total surrender of his spirit into its hands and she would know how false, how inaccurate was the loveless, unloved, unloving spirit of our day and how deep still the fear of love in men. Could she not see now how Hans Taaibosch had proved that this pattern of love was inborn and presided already over the spirit of the first of natural man, and that it was not some civilized or religious afterthought but there full and unafraid from the first point of departure of life on earth?

She protested that she accepted all except that she found it difficult to see how men could be afraid of love. Surely all would naturally welcome it?

The clue to the answer, I replied, was in her instinctive use of the word 'naturally'. Man was too estranged from nature and his natural self to react 'naturally' any more to most circumstances, and least of all to love. He was indeed ready to accept the part of love that pleased him. He was only too eager to exploit it but he was deeply afraid of what it demanded of him in return. It was one of the greatest and subtlest fears not only of our time but of history, hence the crucifixion and the fact that the most accurate symbol of its meaning is still a cross, even if only the cross for a kiss a child puts at the foot of its first inadequate letter home from school in which it has been unable to express its own inexpressible portion of the great hunger that Hans Taaibosch had danced out for her.

I reminded her of how earlier on we had talked about the two which were always necessary for any experience of the living mystery from which our individual sense of meaning came — this 'I' and 'thou' mechanism, this need of a mirror and reflection we needed for recognition of our questing self. This law held good, I believed, even more for love since what love gave to us we had to reflect, to give back in equal measure if it were not to decline and ultimately be withdrawn. It was taking and giving, giving and taking between us and it, that had to be constant. But alas, we tended to want to take in part and give only in part, but it only worked when taken and given in full. It was our fear of the giving back, the change of heart and way of life and total reversal of priorities of values, as well as the discipline and obedience the full return demanded of us, that made us afraid and ultimately caused our shrinking capacity for experiencing it.

I thought it only too appropriate that it took a Roman to deliver the judgement that after what he would have called making love to a woman, a man was sad. Why sad, and not humbled and overawed and filled with a sense of unworthiness of the privilege just conferred? I thought it was because an arrested Roman heart, in that Roman context of worldly power in which it was trapped, could see in that temporary union of feminine and masculine flesh and blood, however close and passionate, only achievement of a mortal end, and not what in effect was the beginning of a calling and a long and singularly exacting apprenticeship to the cause and service of a love that could change his own life and the life of his time out of all recognition, restoring it to the progression of the universe towards the reality of meaning with end. Considering in what a Roman hour of life we too were enclosed, did that help, I asked, anxious in my turn for her answer?

She bowed her head slowly over her hands, clasped and held trembling and so tightly that I saw the skin go white round the knuckles, despite the sheen of light that was like a shawl of silk or gold around her.

Since she did not speak, I assumed the gesture could only be a positive response, and I felt uplifted and encouraged by it. I stress the encouragement because I knew how utterly unrealistic, over-idealistic, indeed laughable all I had said to her would strike a world of men who claimed a monopoly of realism. I believe that it was precisely the unreality of the so-called realism of our time that was lethal to life; because it ignored totally the rule of law of this greatest of realities we had called love. Yet since that too was an essential element of what was to be expected when we left that privileged room and went our separate ways, I thought it as well to warn her of the ridicule and the laughter.

To my amazement, she replied that already she was forewarned and armed against that, thanks to Hans Taaibosch. She said how at first she had been totally put off going to see him perform at the circus because of the way people laughed at him. She described at length how the moment he appeared in the ring, the limelight full on him exposing that strange, protruding behind of his

and round, protuberant stomach, both topped by his archaic little face and odd, black peppercorn head of hair,
the audience would laugh and she could not bear the
quality of the laughter. It made her think of those me-
diaeval crowds who, judging by what she had read, found
hunchbacks, dwarfs and abnormal aberrations of the human form — the greater the abnormality the greater the
fun — cause for endless amusement and superior laughter. And she just could not take it. She would leave outraged as the laughter rose to a greater pitch when Hans
Taaibosch began his antics and dancing. She found
laughter at the attendant clowns bad enough, but they
after all wore the uniform of laughter and were soldiers
enlisted in its service and so prepared for it.

But Hans Taaibosch seemed so naked and unfairly
exposed to it. Yet when she saw him afterwards she found
that, far from having been upset by it, the more he had
been laughed at the more pleased he was and the more
he felt he had succeeded, as if he accepted being laughed
at as his vocation and would have failed his own individual destiny had he not provoked so great a volume of
amusement. Indeed, it was extraordinary to her how im-
measurably his own dignity seemed to increase, how tall
so small a man became in her eyes, by this sheer ac-
ceptance that his vocation was that of making a fool of
himself before others. It was one of the bravest things
she had ever encountered, and after that she herself found
the courage not to shirk watching him in the sawdust
ring when he wished it. Surely there was a lesson in that
for us?

I thanked her, full of an instant and almost overpower-
ing emotion of gratitude for this reminder of how love in
the first instance too would have had to appear as foolishness and its apparent foolishness become part of the

sinister fear of it which I had mentioned, but it was a god-given, divinely inspired foolishness since the increase of love and life depended also on our capacity for allowing ourselves to be made fools of by the as yet untried and unproved meaning. That, I expect, was why St. Paul was so insistent in defining love as neither vain, puffed-up nor proud. I remembered and told her how this too showed Hans Taaibosch to have been an authentic child of mantis because mantis in myth, legend and story had an infinite capacity for foolishness and being made a fool of, both by himself and others, so that we were in the best possible company in this first dimension of love where it appeared dressed up as fool or simpleton.

And so, at last, after what had begun for her with the laughter of Hans Taaibosch in her childhood and ended in a recollection of laughter akin to tears, we came, as I thought mistakenly, to the final level of our reconsideration of the implications of Hans Taaibosch's sojourn among them. I felt free to ask her if she had ever wondered why it was that Hans Taaibosch could have solicited so pure and loyal a love from her? Why was it, as she herself had seen at Pendle Hill and elsewhere, that people who had no experience, pre-knowledge or the most indirect associations with him, his race, history and sombre fate, could yet become so identified with him?

'I can't speak for others, only for myself,' she answered without hesitation and unusual assurance. 'It is quite simple. I just loved him for himself.'

Of course I accepted that implicitly. Yet I had to question whether she had not overlooked this ambivalent principle in life we had talked about so much — this dimension in which we were both ourselves and another, both friend and stranger, brother and enemy, 'I' and 'thou' or perhaps better still in the cooler language of physics, 'mirror' and 'reflection' — this paradoxical organization of all being and things going so deep into the core of even the most inert of substances that, on the last horizons where its infinitessimal constituents were no longer discernible visually but manifest only through the effect of their behaviour on the nuclear constellation of their matter, the sun of their tiny contribution to our physical reality sank into the night still, reflecting and reflected. So that for all of us, Hans Taaibosch was not only himself but also a mirror in which there was also reflection of ourselves. There was the subjective cause of our love and passionate concern for his fate and the fate of his race. There was a Hans Taaibosch in all of us. We too had a cruelly deprived, imperilled natural self. In him and his almost exterminated race, we could see how late the hour was and how urgent the need to succour a natural individual self, bring it across the great divide we had seen so abysmal in the spirit of man, and make it at one with the rest of us which no matter how good the reasons advanced had ruthlessly suppressed it.

For me that was the most urgent, the truly realistic task which contemporary man faced. If this reconciliation were not effected wholly and with equal honour and respect for both of these great opposites in man, human life would be torn further apart than ever between two partial and self-cancelling expressions of itself. I had put the burden on the individual because that, I believed, was the only way all real change begins in life. This love, this improbable calling for wholeness in life, had to be experienced first in loneliness and isolation by a single heart and lived out in the small round of one unique life, however powerless and absurd it may appear to itself, before the great impersonal and arrogant collective spirit of our time would be moved to imitate it. That was always how real change in history began; one heart truly turned in the direction of wholeness and the movement of life and the universe itself conformed in due course. Just as physics found the greatest source of energy today in the smallest unit of matter, the atom, so the smallest unit of man, the individual atom, nuclear in this division between the Jacob and Esau in himself but contained in love, was the greatest force of change in human societies.

The symbol and the images in which this greater self pursued us were always more than any dogma, theory or imagination could express. The answers it sought had to be lived before they could be known. So the time for exhortation, dogma and hair-splitting words had gone; a time had come when only a true example of love accurately re-experienced and lived in an individual round of life could open up the collective life of our time for the re-entry of love and submission to the rule of the greatest law of creation. For creation was growth, slow, patient, enduring and endless. There were no short cuts to it. The idea that there were intellectual, wilful, short cuts to any real change for the better was one cause of the barbarism and violence increasingly in command of the spirit of our time. The longest way round was the shortest way to creative change and such a change possible only as a process of growth in keeping with the law of time which I had already defined also as the patience of love. I would even go so far as to say that the future of human life depended on the rate at which such individual examples could be achieved, made manifest and multiplied.

That is why the individual example of love fulfilled on a cross two thousand years ago continued to haunt us so, despite all our evasions and excellent reasons produced for dismissing its significance, and would go on haunting us until we too as the single spies that had to precede the battalions to come, re-discovered a love as complete. In the profoundest of senses that one crucified example was a life fulfilled not in the remote past but still far ahead of us in the future, because we had not caught up with it yet. It was indeed even more of a futuristic than an historical reality. How tragic but how true that there had only been one modern man, and he had been killed two thousand years ago for the love that made him for ever immediate. But to make this great universal specific in all that had been resurrected of love between us in that room in the person of Hans Taaibosch, he in his own small way seemed to me to have testified in a manner no cross-examination could shake, to the power of love through this metamorphosis of his Stone-Age self.

Accordingly let us remember above all how, just as she in sculpting him had given him the vital act of recognition necessary for giving him back his own inborn dignity in life, he enabled us to recognize our own persecution of a natural self hungry for love and a place in a life of love. The sooner we gave it the kind of love she had given Hans Taaibosch and brought it out into the light of day, the sooner would begin the arrest of this spread of the impersonal, conformist collective obsessions of our day, so formidable that it was like a proliferation of uniform cells in a cancer of our time. Could she not see how approximate and inaccurate human life was becoming and how it was not a unity but a paralysing generalization, which eliminated life-giving differences and concealed a terrible, dispirited fragmentation of unloved selves underneath?

I hoped she would realize how here least of all I used the term love in any sentimental, loose or lush a state. I was thinking here above all of love as the act of the

The Carol

knowledge of the totality to come, not a cerebral knowing but the emotion of a knowing before the fact of it, charged with awareness of all the life that had ever been, was and could be. It demanded therefore also that we should know ourselves as it knew us in the full term of our origin and destination. It demanded that we should make knowing and accepting responsibility for all of ourselves, without fear or favour for any part of ourselves, the foremost and most urgent of our tasks. In return it would do the rest.

This was precisely why, I was convinced, Hans Taaibosch meant so much to her and he and his people to me, because they reflected a critical area of injury and neglect in ourselves, our societies and cultures. Otherwise we could not have cared so much and would not have had to go on caring since we too were born to be raised as loyal subjects of love imperative, demanding to be lived whole through us.

STRANGE JERUSALEM

Strange Jerusalem

I AM not sure, so long ago was it now, but I believe that it was with some such words as those that we ended our consideration of the conception, birth, life, death and resurrection of the vanished and obscure Hans Taaibosch, unrecorded in the annals of his country and memory of his people, as I was to find after the most prolonged searching in the years that followed. All the places I was to visit which once must have known him so well, knew and remembered him no more. And yet two significant facts were to emerge. They were the result of one of the last things this woman uttered to me on parting.

It was a single, simple request, ardent enough to become a command. As I escorted her out into the street to get a cab for her, we stood for a while silent, side by side, looking up and down the broad avenue unusually swollen with traffic. We could not alas see the night sky which we knew to be winter clear and full of stars, because we were there so deep on the floor of a canyon among the peaks of glass and steel of this high sierra city of New York. We noticed how bravely the Christmas illuminations maintained their unworldly purpose in that worldly setting of such masterful proportions. I was instantly moved by it. I thought at first it was because of my own many and in some ways singular associations with the coming

161

A Mantis Carol

event. But I soon realized that there was more to my
reaction than ever before. A new element had come to
dominate it. It was simply this, that if the birth of spring
in the darkest hour of the year was coincident with the
re-birth of the principle of love some two thousand years
ago, so that time, through its own movement and character would reinforce its growth and make of it a spring
also in the spirit of man, giving it so much meaning for
enough people to compel the vast city into celebrating it
thus with light, I was looking then into the heart of what
had been Jerusalem to Hans Taaibosch.

Hard on that, when I was helping her towards her cab,
characteristically not thinking of herself or her own feelings but still of that uncared-for fragment of the image
of deprived being who had come in so strange a guise
into her life in search of love and for a while had taken
on as one of the many names under which it has conducted its long search for shelter, that of Hans Taaibosch,
she asked in a low, urgent voice, 'Will you please promise
to give Hans's love to the desert when you go back in
the New Year?'

I promised, and the promise remained uppermost with
me amid all the turmoil of mind over my departure and
flight back home, where I wanted to be with my own family
for Christmas. It was with me when high over the Western ocean towards the end of that day of our separation
a great night rushed to meet us. I sat with my face pressed
to the window watching star after star emerge full and
clear and precise as I had never seen them, until there
hardly seemed room for any more in the sky, and all the
stars, altogether without exception, seemed to be shaking
and trembling and as if dancing all over that smooth,
black floor of Heaven to the beat of one of Hans Taaibosch's
renderings of the dance of the great hunger.

And watching them thus, hour after hour, I was aware of another level which that woman and I had not yet considered; the gratitude to life which comes flooding in over one as one experiences again how pervasive and always near is this mystery of love as though it were delegate in the blood and bone of ourselves. For such a gratitude was flooding me unsolicited from within, giving me so intense a feeling of belonging and participation in the movement and activity of the stars that I was dazzled with the light as of certain knowledge. I had an emotion of knowing beyond doubt how, long before we were thought of or conceived and the dancing stars made, already all was loved, and that however provisional or inadequate the shape in which it was expressed at any given moment in time, despite the apparent ruthlessness of the inevitable processes of dissolution involved, all would be as carefully, lovingly and tenderly unshaped, the stars unmade and the universe dismantled as in their fashioning at the beginning, since in the instant of undoing, unmaking and dismantling, all would be reborn and remade into a greater expression of the love that is our origin and destination.

I remember that as this gratitude and the sense of infinite but undeserved grace produced by it moved me to tears, I thought how significant then was the last in the long series of coincidences I have mentioned and that I should happen to be flying at that very moment due East out of which the new morning was to come. I was compelled through this, as if it were part of the meaning intended in the experience behind me by the first cause of it all, to recall an incident in the evolution of mantis, the god of Hans Taaibosch. After one of his greatest dreams had delivered him and his family from extinction in a perilous encounter with evil, in the titanic proportions of

an element Hans Taaibosch's people call the 'all-de-
vourer', mantis had gathered his strange little company
close around him. Still shaken by their near delivery from
elimination, they looked around themselves and saw the
long, tasselled green-gold grass of a vast Kalahari summer, shot and shadowy with silk of a newly risen wind,
the wind which is forever charged to bear the image of
the spirit in search of the meaning we call love. And that
wind, too, was coming out of the East. Instantly, so the
remnants of Hans Taaibosch's people told me, all knew
that the dreaming of mantis had not failed them, their
hearts no longer were full of fear and their tears of distress
left them.

And so in this and other various ways, the feeling of
being a carrier of a message of love from Hans Taaibosch
remained with me on a series of long journeys that led
to my return to the heart of the desert. And though, as
I have said, I found no trace or shadow of memory of
him in the desert, I discovered that taking the thought
of his love there as commanded by the woman who had
loved him, the scene looked different to me, although I
had known it well enough before. It was as if I were
looking at it with my eyes opened to a wider vision, as
happens when one sees a landscape, no matter how fa-
miliar, after confrontation with a rendering of it by a new,
great and inspired painter, and is humbled and somewhat
outraged by the realization of how small a shift of position
in our wilful senses it took to make accessible such un-
suspected riches of shape, colour and rhythm in what
had appeared an exhausted view for so long.

Even I, for whom the desert was no spent reality and
who had always possessed an unaccountable and inexpressible love of it, was overcome by the change and
realized I had never known how, despite all appearances

to the contrary, it had also been fashioned in the fullness of love long before it was made or Hans Taaibosch born. And fashioned thus moreover so as to become a sort of refuge for a first exercise of love, where an essential element of it could be kept alive, even if only in the unlikely shape of insects like mantis and his enigmatic bird, animal and rainbow friends, to tend to an ember of it, so that when life in a world otherwise so abundant failed it outside, one could return there for means of rekindling its fire, and that in some sort of semblance such as this was concealed the aboriginal purpose of a wasteland not only in the physical world but also in the spirit of man.

Yes, in bringing Hans Taaibosch's vicarious message of love to the desert from a great city that knew it not, it was as if with the storm clouds of summer standing like monuments and towers and battlements of marble so high in the trembling blue above it, I saw a certainty of promise that the garden in the beginning, no matter how far lost behind us now, could be recovered through love and the desert we had made of it redeemed. So, when after the night the first rain fell, that rain which is for ever the image of love in action, the immense, scorched, Cinderella earth, so full of the great hunger, conceived and within days was transformed with new life of grass, flowers and budding thorn, and resounded with the drumming of bees making honey and the singing of birds building nests, I thought I had never seen a greater statement of beauty in my own round of life on earth. And I knew as never before that there was no greater beauty possible in nature or man than that of the uncared for and rejected, rediscovered and redeemed for growth through love.

Consequently, I turn to it all to this day whenever

165

assailed by doubt, as a sailor to his compass on a night of storm, finding redirection in this magnetic testimony to the inescapable pursuit and transforming power of love, not forgetting that none of this would have been possible had it not been for the appearance of mantis, the great dreamer himself, in the dream of a sleeping woman, and remembering above all how unerringly the dream, dreaming through him and her, had led to this discovery of the manifestation of the power of love in the wasteland which is a modern city, so pure and convincing that I have been compelled by nature of my own calling to record it here also as a memorial of the dreamer, the dream and those who had lived it against all the improbable odds of our desperate day, just for the love of it.